"Quality is Everything!"

by

Ken D. Walston, Jr.

This book is the explicit expression and dedicated work of the author, who is considered to be a Subject Matter Expert (SME) in the field and science of Quality Assurance, Quality Engineering and Quality Management.

The sole purpose in the publication of this book, is to give the reader an education and insightful knowledge to the importance of Quality as viewed from an Expert; based on industrial experience, decades of hands-on application, mentoring and pedigree to reveal without any question or doubt that, "Quality is Everything!"

ISBN Softcover 978-0-692-17525-5

PUBLISHED BY
Walston & Associates
www.walstonassociates.com

Printed in the United States of America

Dedicated to

This book is dedicated to the two most influential gentlemen and mentors in my career path.
Mr. Daniel P. Hybner and Dr. W. Edwards Deming

Both men are no longer with us: but have an everlasting impact on the discipline related to Quality and created a sense of profound assurance, which allows me to proclaim that,

"Quality is Everything!"

BY THE AUTHOR'S REQUEST

The end of this book has a Special Insight and Synopsis, called the LASTWORD written by a gentleman named George Rule.

George Rule is a close associate of the Author and a highly skilled Quality Professional, with over thirty years in the Science and Application of Quality, with a diverse tenure of experience.

He is highly regarded amongst colleagues as a mentor and teacher and holds his own notoriety within this field; he is a man of impeccable honor, ethics and distinction.

Mr. Rule is a retired Naval Officer and Veteran of twenty-two years, with assignments as electronics officer, combat systems officer, and Tactical Data Systems officer in major combatant ships.

Subsequent to this, he joined the Aerospace Defense Industry working for three major Aerospace corporations as a Quality Engineer and very quickly moved into Quality Management.

George holds certifications from the American Society for Quality as a Certified Quality Engineer as well as a Certified Software Quality Engineer. He has a lifetime California Community College Teaching Credential in Engineering and Business under Industrial Management.

George is currently retired and resides in Southern California.

George Rule

INTRODUCTION

"Quality is Everything" has been a mantra that I've been preaching and practicing for the last thirty-five years.

I've based an entire career in Quality, from Middle Management through the Executive Levels.

I've cut my teeth with some of the biggest Fortune 100 Corporations in the United States (commercial, aerospace, space, and Department of Defense) and on some of the most profound, State-of-the-Art programs ever conceived.

It eventually led me into a business venture (Walston & Associates) where I could help design architectural improvements in "Quality" for businesses who were having problems with Non-Conformances and Supplier Quality issues, Quality Improvement Techniques, and the mandatory effort in becoming ISO/AS9100 Registrar Certified.

Through these years I've seen the discipline of my career evolve in fashion with technology, industrial settings, institutional models, political correctness, and oxymoron ideologies. "Quality" hasn't always been Everything to a lot of businesses out there.

My experience and pedigree reject the layman theology about Quality, as just being "Common Sense".

The field of Quality is a science, and the applied protocols and methods of Quality are quantitative, precise and a "Value Added" resource when implemented throughout a business infrastructure.

The same holds true for each of us as individuals in our life's journey.

The Quality mindset enhances organizing, making fewer mistakes, making sound decisions, acquiring better products and services, self-improvement, better communications…all in all, a more disciplined self.

I want to explore with you what "Quality" really is, from a personal everyday experience, into the professional industrial work setting of Quality Assurance and possibly some conservative perspectives.

"Quality" is one of the most (if not the most) misunderstood and bastardized word in the English Language.

In an industrial setting it exceeds the Norm of Expectations.

Even though we Americans purchase more products from foreign manufactured sources and distributors through a seemingly endless supply from super discounted warehouse stores, we still love a good yard sale or flea market and are always looking for the best buy at the lowest price.

We expect the Highest Quality of the products we so cheaply buy and demand higher value and quantity in the same breath.

"I want the Best Bang for my Buck" is the Great American Motto.

Is that greed or just a value minded thinking?

Do we Americans need to get back to the basic principles that we had from the Post WWII Era into the 1950s and 60s?

A time when credit wasn't so easily accessible, and you didn't purchase more than you could afford. Deficit spending hadn't hit the average American household way of life yet.

That the value of a dollar directly equated to the Quality and craftsmanship of the product you purchased or are we okay with "more for my buck" and compromising Quality for the sheer volume that you can carry away or even consume.

As we currently live in the third and are moving towards the fourth decade of the 21st Century, America is now more self-serving, self-consumed and porky than ever before.

Porky, in having the highest obesity rates nationwide ever (especially among children).

It's all that cheap, high sodium, high fat and mega preservative fast-food America consumes by the tons each year.

I mention this along with the porky reference because 1) it's a prominent issue within our society, and 2) the perception of Quality is really not being considered with health and a situation like obesity, which is usually the direct result of poor eating habits and the lack of a regimented exercise program and lifestyle (self-discipline).

Note to reference: There are many individuals who legitimately suffer from a medical condition or linked to possible genetics who are chronically overweight or obese. The reference here to Porky is not meant to be associated to those individuals. Unfortunately, the majority of obesity and overweight conditions are immediately claimed as medical or genetic, when in reality they are self induced by social and discipline disorders. That in my opinion is just laziness and an extremely unhealthy condition, which will not impart a good Quality of Life to any individual.

For decades now, we have been totally obsessed with our body and physical fitness that career paths and industries have been marketed out of it.

The marketing aspect has exploited glamour much more than health.

There is no doubt that everyone should have physical exercise in their life each and every day and that maintaining a certain individual body fat count can be a healthy thing; but the extent of obsession with the physical for our body is beyond normal.

Obsession is a form of addiction and becomes very unhealthy mentally and results in many individuals losing personal control of their life path and become reliant on artificial stimulus to secure their happiness and sense of well-being.

Having a "little" bit more fat is just as beneficial as having a "little" less fat in the diet, but excess in any form of intake or expulsion for a human is not a prescribed trait.

Yet obesity is predicted to remain as the biggest disease-causing attribute and number one contributor to health care cost in the 21st Century.

Aside from this, yet within the same vein, is our obsession with environmental issues which have gone way beyond good science and into the realm of pure speculation and political agendas.

Again, present and future career paths and industries have been marketed out of this.

And again, the agenda is to exploit fear and spread false propaganda for political gain about global warming and imminent global disasters.

We've had forty years of bad science and bad experts predicting the Polar Ice Caps melting causing global flooding, the earth warming to a constant global ambient temperature, massive crop and species eliminations, devastating Green House affects to where the earth will become like Venus, no more winters or maybe another Ice Age, Polar Bears and Seals moving into beach side communities because all the ice bergs have melted; and it goes on and on... it has been difficult to substantiate by real expert scientists working in the fields of Meteorology, Climatology or Oceanography who don't have a political agenda to support.

What is happening on the earth right now in regional weather changes is not unique to the earth's history. The Star that is 93 million miles away from us has 99% of the control over our weather and any "So Called" Climate change occurring. As well, we are starting to go through a slow but ever-changing Polar Shift. Our Magnetic Poles are starting to shift from North to South. This too is not unique in the earth's history, even to the point at which we have in our history, lost complete magnetic flux on the earth for short periods of time. It has happened multiple times throughout the evolution of this planet. All of these things are occurring right now since mankind has been in existence on this planet, or since mankind has been able to record events taking place since our existence, so it seems unique to us.

On top of this, is the restless anxiety of our economy and the personal impact it has on each and every person living in America and around the world; it's a global disaster.

From the national scene, we Americans have had this out-of-control spending mentality, joined with an uncontrollable desire to accumulate more and more personal and material wealth through credit, than ever before in our history.

Is this our obsession to reach a higher Quality of Life?

If it was, then we would have higher moral values and less need for temporal gratification.

As self-gratification becomes more prevalent, moral values decrease and the desire to work as a collective People (Nation) is stifled.

National solidarity becomes less desirable and gives prevalence to political and social insurrections.

We become totally divided and split into cultural and political diversities, eventually fighting for each group's rights and privileges and then turning against the sum of the whole.

In order to give some concessions before we declare all out war on each other, we embrace the philosophy of Tolerance or Co-Existence.

Quality of Life is not something you can purchase towards, it is establishing inner peace and obtaining and maintaining control of your life space.

It's really about how you spend your time, energy and resources towards living at ease within your environment.

All indications show that we have a new national passion with Greed. It's an old desire but has come back into fruition.

We've gone from Deficit Spending comparisons in hundreds of millions to billions and now into trillions.

Back in the late 1950's and early 1960's there was a popular television show called, "The Millionaire".

The theme of the show was about a guy who would give away some of his fortune to whomever he considers to be a worthy recipient. He'd donate one million dollars to the lucky individual.

Now, at that time in America, one million dollars was an astronomical amount of money to the common citizen and viewed as the monetary figure equating what rich was.

It would be the equivalent of what "Entertainment Tonight" posts these days as the Top Richest Individuals in America. In a matter of five decades, that equivalent moved towards being a Billionaire.

It is important to realize that a Billion is a thousand million.

The jump here is quite significant in figures being exponential and time being so short.

It used to be that corporations were rated to be worth billions of dollars, now it's the standard for status of individuals and the new goal for our children to set their sights on.

Something has greatly gone astray in America when the expectations of Corporate CEO's are to go from single digit million-dollar bonuses to double digits and outsource more services and business offshore to make bigger profits and justify their decisions based on increasing self gratuity.

In contrast, the expectation of the workers below on the food chain is maxing out with 3% merit increases (and that's the best performers), with some getting nothing. The rate for considering compensation with merit is based on a Bell Curve, so some get the max amount available in the pool of monies designated and some get zero.

Notwithstanding, in dire times cutbacks and even lay-offs are the "Call to Arms" for most businesses and corporations in order to maintain or meet the forecasted profit margins, that's Standard Business Operations (SBO).

Wall Street and those stockholders get very nervous if their Investment Trades are in jeopardy of losing a single penny, if that occurs then the "Call to Arms" is...Sell! Sell! Sell!

The CEOs however keep their bonuses as does the upper tier of Executive Management.

In the 2008 National and Global Banking Crisis our national banking and financial institutions were failing and falling by the wayside at record high levels and Wall Street was whining like a 747 over dropping below twelve thousand on the Dow Jones.

The Big Desperate Act for recovery was to pump hundreds of billions of Taxpayers money from the U.S. Treasury, into bailing out major corporate banks, financial institutions and select industrial corporations. Instead of letting the Capitalistic Strategy take over and let them declare bankruptcy or go out of business, which would have evened the playing field and allowed competition to ease and strengthen the Recovery.

As history has eventually showed, the "Obama Recovery Plan" didn't work, it only made it worse with a GDP of 1.3% and unemployment at 7.8% when he finally left office in 2016.

Now as this book is being written, under the second term of the Trump Administration, we are diverting another big economic disaster recovery type like that of 2008 and the Post-Depression Era of the 1930's, with the Dow at record breaking Highs (46K-47K+) on the exchange and over 69 Million Share Trades per day, and unemployment at 4.1, a drop from 7.1%, in 2024 under the Biden Administration.

Nevertheless, with all of this fabulous increase in national financial prosperity and unemployment, it only helps increase the "Profit" mentality and does not help with looking at "Quality" instead of Quantity. You cannot equate the two as being the same.

Quality suffers at all levels of our society when outrageous projected forecasts and profit margins run the business decisions and Wall Street runs the country.

Even with a great Mantra such as, Make America Great Again, the corporate mindset moves away from "Quality is Everything" towards Cost or Profit is Everything.

Don't let anyone fool you with the standard comeback, "We are finding ways of working Smarter" when it comes to cutbacks and digging deep to reduce cost.

More entrepreneur consulting agencies and Institutions of Quality Improvement popped up out of the 1980's and 90s because of the idea of working Smarter as a means to reduce head count and cut costs for bigger profits.

More than in any other time in the Modern Industrial Age, monster concepts like Quality Circles and the "Big Q" methodologies brought many businesses into ruin, by spending hundreds of thousands of dollars to incorporate silly Quality Improvement Programs.

Much of these required added personnel to develop Data Systems and expensive software, to collect mega-bites of data for reports and metrics, which in turn, did nothing but create bureaucratic support groups (departments) and destroy the already working infrastructure.

Please don't get me wrong, as a Quality Professional, I am not advocating No Quality Metrics or not implementing Quality Improvement measures.

These are greatly needed like a Cost of Poor Quality System (COPQ) and Trend Metrics, or a Corrective and Preventative Action (CAPA) System.

These kinds of things must be implemented in order to drill down the reasons of the root cause to defects and anomalies...but to Institutionalize QA or the aspects of Quality, is asinine.

My foremost philosophy is: K.I.S.S. (Keep It Simple Stupid).

The Stupid part is if you allow it to become so complex that nothing gets done in the Processes of Improvement.

Like the Toyota (TPS) Process to be implemented (Full Blown), or the EU Version of QRQC, in an Aerospace Manufacturing Company. It is so costly and inappropriate, yet American Aerospace Corporations, in an attempt to be Global Savvy and compliant, have been implementing and conforming to something that has transformed the American Business Models into an EU and Asian compliant structure.

The Quality Experts that are pushing this have a big share in the profit they will be collecting in the millions of dollars it will take to incorporate through consultants and years of total business restructuring.

Misguided and misunderstood, with visions of Mega-Dollar insight, these Corporate CEOs have been drinking the

Globalization Kool-Aid thinking that it will increase their market share, when in reality it has increased their cost of doing business in the Global Market. These concepts were introduced into American Corporate structures by the EU Nations alone with the Japanese auto industry in order to advance their Technology and Quality concepts and increase their share of infiltrating American Industries to buy and control.

Another misconception in adding to the Profit Margin is Cutting Costs. This more than not impacts Quality.

You just can't cut costs thinking that you are improving Quality.

It's how these cuts are imposed as improvements, trimming the fat and not cutting into the muscle.

When this supersedes our ability to produce, then businesses go "Out of Business!"

Cost cuts must be identifying the areas of waste and eliminating that first and foremost.

What's the purpose of having Quality Improvement measures if not to identify and reduce wasteful Scrap, Rework and Warranty expenditures.

From the American Corporate Management perspective, the easiest way with the highest and fastest visibility results for Cost Reductions is to reduce headcount.

What usually and most often is not done is to eliminate the wasteful conditions after the layoffs have occurred.

So, you still have the hundreds of thousands, even millions of dollars in wasteful practices and processes still in place; so, in reality all that has happened is a "Show for the Moment".

All of us as consumers naturally feed our addiction to purchasing what we want in any way which is affordable.

If we can't buy local or buy American because businesses have shut down or gone offshore, then we start buying goods and acquire services outside of our internal national setting and go offshore to countries where products and services can be rendered cheaper; but look out, the Quality is usually not there.

With this, the Quality of Life, Quality of Intellect, Quality of Goods and Services, Quality of Expectations is altered and our perception of these becomes perverse.

It's all been shrouded in the privilege called the "American Dream", whose origin was based on the concept of an individual's ability to succeed (*the Sky's the Limit*), through hard work, blood, sweat and tears.

Where "No Bars Hold" afforded any citizen of the United States the assurance of Life, Liberty and the Pursuit of Happiness.

Our Federal Republic was not founded on the concept of democracy or receiving something for nothing.

It wasn't established or ratified on a political or social agenda of welfare or distributing individual wealth evenly to the masses (Socialism).

The concept of America, which has been so attractive to everyone in the world, was its Rights to Freedom, within the statues of Law and Justice, represented by the People and for the People.

It was our "Free Enterprise" Capitalistic System strategy that helped us become the world's leader with Commerce and Industry, in and through the last century.

This affords the privilege of giving endless opportunities for anyone to succeed and places no limits on that success.

The outcome is a high and sustainable Quality of Life. This is the "American Dream".

Perhaps the bigger issue for this generation may be that the "Buy Now" with credit concept has given way to a new cultural lifestyle. A very damaging Lifestyle.

A generation has been born out of it, which doesn't see "NO" as part of their behavioural discipline.

Where whatever you want is a right to be given to you (Endowment or Entitlement) and walking away with products and obtaining services has no consequence towards payment of the debt.

America has embraced a false god, called GREED!

WALSTON RULE #1
"Quality is Everything!"

The term "Quality" is synonymous with expecting the "Very Best of".

If you wanted to define what the intent of Quality is, I've concluded that it is- *the measurement of performance against a standard, to the degree of excellence which qualifies the outcome of any given function or process by which something is produced or created.*

I suppose a Divine example of this could be found in Genesis 1:31, "and God looked upon all that He had created and saw that it was very good" (*He was very pleased*).

This conclusion of "Very Good" that God expressed would be based upon a standard that He had set for measuring what Quality Excellence was from one point (His Perspective) to another point of measuring that Perspective (the Physical Creation).

The model or standard was already in place before the conclusion could be given. God had a basis of coming to His conclusion because the standard model for judging it was before Him and was established to be the standard to which all things would be measured against.

Therefore, the Quality of what was created was considered the "Very Best of" due to the fact that it met the requirements of the standard it was created from.

Bringing this down to earth, if this example was reflective of a manufacturing process or product-line, we would say that the product was "Built to Print". The Build to Print perception is that the product meets the approved design characteristics as outlined on a drawing or model layout and functionality as tested to the design criteria, then manufactured with the finished product meeting the end-users Quality expectations and satisfaction.

Thus, a guarantee or warranty is issued to serve as an assurance of complete Customer Satisfaction through purchasing the product or obtaining a service.

Why does a manufacturer give a guarantee or warranty on products?

It's because if they are produced to a higher Quality Standard, the risk of failure or defect is very low, and the risk of return is close to null before the guarantee period has expired.

It is a selling point for customer satisfaction which equates to the end-user believing that "Quality is Everything!"

Even though the word "Quality" may not be mentioned, in the mind of the Consumer the term is implied.

How does the average person truly look at what they are buying?

Nine times out of ten, if asked, you'll hear, "I want the Best Quality at the Lowest Price."

Every once in a while, you'll get someone express a euphemism like, "Quality? You get what you pay for."

Nevertheless, those individuals also want the Best Quality at the Best Price.

Experience shows us that this is the ponderous mindset of most Americans, so our desire for the best at the cheapest is an oxymoron.

How many people actually buy something without first looking at the price and that is the factor which is their final persuasion in buying that particular product.

Be honest with yourself...

When we purchase something, make or manufacture something, sell or trade something; aren't we looking for and judging the Quality of it in every aspect?

If we compromise and disregard the Quality for Price, then we have already determined our acceptance of the product without meeting our Standard for Quality and are not really disappointed when it breaks or doesn't last too long.

In 2016, prior to the Presidential Election, I conducted a physical poll from a survey I had devised of nineteen questions.[1]

The intent was to gather data from a live and random forum, where the population is most diverse in order to get an average impression of people's buying habits and if their perspective towards Quality was one of the considerations.

This information was put into a spreadsheet where trend data could be produced and analyzed.

I chose two hundred and fifty people at random locations within the Metro San Francisco and Los Angeles areas, totaling a sample of five hundred people.

My attempt was to make it as diverse across racial, cultural and economic lines as possible.

This was done at shopping malls and food supermarkets.

I conducted a second physical poll in 2017 after the Presidential Election of another five hundred people from the same Metro areas within different locations with the same intent to sample individuals across diverse racial, cultural and economic lines as possible.

This was done at car dealerships ranging within the economy to luxury styles from Ford, GM, Mercedes, Toyota, KIA, BMW, Honda and Volkswagen.

Finally, in late 2017 I conducted a third Internet Poll using Professional Networking sites I was associated with, which were from individuals and locations within the United States and around the world.

The issue from my perspective was getting a well-rounded participation from the demographic base I had chosen to take the survey.

As it turned out with the physical survey, Anglo and African Americans were more receptive to the survey than were Hispanic, Asian or other groups interviewed.

[1] Appendix A - Walston & Associates Quality Survey © 2016-2017

Apart from answering the standard survey questions, there were many instances (eighty percent or more) where the surveyor was able to have generalized conversations with those surveyed.

As an additive to the evaluation and conclusions regarding this survey, those conversations, mixed with the surveyors' own professional and life experiences and interpretations thereof are used.

What the data showed was an Absolute Trend.[2]

Ninety-five percent of the Anglo and African Americans were born in the United States and lived their entire life in the U.S., in comparison to seventy percent of the Hispanic and forty-five percent of the Asians who were born in the United States.

In contrast, only five percent of the Anglo and African Americans were born outside of the United States, while thirty percent of Hispanic and fifty-five percent of Asians were born outside of the United States and only lived part of their adulthood in the U.S.

Foreign Nationals or persons living in the United States on Work Visas or Green Cards, were also participants in the survey.

Thirty-five percent were Hispanic, twenty percent Asian and forty-five percent Hindu (India) claimed to be documented aliens; all (100%) were working in the United States.

With the Internet Polling (I), slightly over five thousand working class professionals (ranging from CEOs, Vice-Presidents, Managers, IT Engineers, Design Engineers, Banking Professionals, Software Specialists, etc) were sent the survey with (61 %) completing it.

It gave a very interesting perspective in counterbalancing how professional working-class individuals in the United States viewed the question of Quality, verses professional working classes in other countries.

[2] Appendix B – Walston & Associates Quality Survey Metrics © 2017

Fifty-seven percent were Anglo (White) followed by twenty-three percent foreign nationals and the next highest group being Asian, with the largest percentage between the ages of 31-40 and respective mean income between $81K- $100K annually.[2]

In contrast to the Physical Poll (P), eighty percent of the Anglo's were born in the United States, ninety-eight percent of Black, ninety-five percent of Hispanic and fifty-five percent of Asians were born in the United States; none of the Hindu's polled were U.S. born [2]

Out of the Physical Polling five percent were unemployed.

Due to the mechanism of the Internet Polling, we were able to deduce that the Foreign Nationals were ninety-nine percent working in the U.S., eighty-five percent Hindu (India), twelve percent Asian and two percent Hispanic[2], but not able for the U.S. born surveyed.

(P) 1000 Individuals Surveyed
(I) 3035 Individuals Completed Survey

| | U.S. BORN | | FOREIGN NATIONALS | | MALE / FEMALE RATIO | | | |
					Male	Female	Male	Female
	(P)	(I)	(P)	(I)	(P)		(I)	
Anglo	95%	80%	0%	0%	65%	35%	55%	45%
Black	95%	98%	0%	0%	75%	25%	85%	15%
Hispanic	70%	95%	35%	1%	35%	65%	95%	5%
Asian	45%	55%	20%	12%	65%	35%	75%	25%
Hundu (India)	0%	0%	45%	85%	100%	0%	80%	20%

The most important aspect under consideration, is questioning if the increased diversity of our cultural group settings is having an affect on Quality in the United States.

In contrast to what Post WWII America was eighty years ago to now, our politics, religious centricity, moral attitude and Justice System have shifted from "Middle of the Road", "Right Wing" Conservative to "Radical", "Left Wing Ideolog" Liberal.

[2] Appendix B – Walston & Associates Quality Survey Metrics © 2017

All of these have dramatically influenced and changed what our current lifestyles have become.

It has introduced political correctness, compromise and relaxed every aspect of our society's concept of Quality and expectations of what "Good" is, or at least should be.

A big share in this is partly due to a large and consistent influx of refugee populations from Asia (in particular Southeast Asia starting in the Mid 1970's), Central and South America and Eastern Europe after the end of the Cold War Era and fall of the Soviet Union in the early 1990's. But today, we have an influx of millions of illegal immigrants into the United States which are not educated nor productive of usable skill sets in order to add any Value-Added Resource to our society, business structures or national security. In fact, all of these things are depleted because of a direct result of it.

The IT and .com boom of the 1990's brought an on-slot of Chinese and Hindu immigration and the beginning of offshore and outsourcing human resources to fill Hi-Tech and Internet recruiting into the United States.

For the first time in our history China was producing more Engineering Graduates than the United States.

From 2004 through 2008, the estimates were that five hundred thousand engineers per year were coming out of Asia and a large majority of these are being recruited by corporations in the United States.

From 2005-2010, New Zealand saw an opportunity to grab a huge entrepreneur piece of the explosion from Asia and invested in building an infrastructure to house and educate foreign nationals in learning English, so they could be more competitive in the western markets.

They spent millions of dollars creating an infrastructure, building student communities of housing flats, to house thousands of Asian students for trade school programmes with full English curriculums.

We boast as being a nation of immigrants, but the infiltration of mass offshore non-educated and unskilled migration, and especially illegal immigrants, has increased sub-cultural dissidents within our major inner-city population and inadvertently allowed unlawful forms of activities and illegal population growth to settle in.

There has always been a convoluting of the Illegal Immigration issue in America due to our liberal migration policies and lack of law enforcement, especially from Mexico into the Southwestern United States and California.

Within this region, it has reached epidemic proportions because of our open border access and smuggling availability of illegal contraband as well as people.

The assimilation of these populations into our society has never been successfully coordinated by the Federal, State or Local governments to fit a national (American) life-style caricature.

In each of these scenarios, what is created are individual sub-cultural communities with some obvious names which help identify their place of origin, such as; Little Italy, Little Saigon, China Town, Korea Town, Little TJ, etc.

These bring their native homeland customs with them in every aspect of language, food, religion, hygiene, politics, and Quality of lifestyle.

Whether or not this is adversely opposed to the established American lifestyle, ethics and laws embraced by the majority of citizens within the United States; in time, the numbers of these cultural diversities will change the sense of Quality, from a single Standard of measurement into diverse cultural measures.

The training, intellect and workmanship skill set is also questionable.

The amount of rework and scrap, and their associated costs, are proportionate due to these factors.

Immigration in America is greatly needed and welcomed when it can be uniformly applied throughout the established Laws and Legal Process into Citizenship and Common American Culture.

The culture in turn, must be based upon a Common Language, Political System, Social Justice and Law.

When diversity is equated as the mixture of sub-cultures and communities, being allowed to infiltrate on an established societies common culture, within existing customs and national heritage, then history shows us that what occurs is social and civil unrest.

Opposing ideologies and debate, especially of a cultural nature, can be substantiated in civil manner when the outcome is towards the improvement and common good of sustaining the established national heritage, traditions and government.

A good example of this is where we are starting to see more and more outward display of another nation's flag taking precedence above the Stars and Stripes.

Federal Law prohibits a foreign national flag to be placed above the American National Flag in public display.

What we are seeing in the border states of the southwestern United States is just that.

Businesses are flying the national flag of Mexico above the U.S. National Flag.

A lot of private citizens who are Veterans are outraged and taking matters into their own hands by ripping down these flags from public view.

Large groups of protestors holding banners, calling for equality under Mexican Law and also holding the national flag of Mexico as the banner of their alliance.

What we are seeing is the beginning of incitement into Civil Unrest and eventually confrontation.

The diversity of One World uniformity is not going to fit into the Traditional American Constitution and established ideologies of traditional American Society.

It is something that will require insurgent-revolutionary tactics from both social uprising and political propaganda. It is beginning by changing our history and heritage.

The American Institution as propagated since the Revolutionary War in 1775 will not stand for our national Heritage and Freedom's to be stolen, taken away or reduced...we may through greed or ignorance allow our standard for Quality to degrade, but not our Freedom!

The United States of America is a Federal Republic, governed by a Ratified Constitution and Bill of Rights.

We are a "Free" Nation, a Federal Republic and not a Democracy.

We are unique among all other nations on the earth.

Our Forefather's and the Founders of our Constitution brought forth a nation to be endowed by the Rule of Law and to be governed by the Will of the People and not by the government..." For the People, by the People"

All Federal elected officials and military personnel take a sworn oath to uphold and defend the Constitution of the United States...anything less than, is treason.

Funny thing about that word "Defend", it implies, to give your life for.

Freedom affects the outcome of "Quality", as does an oppressive environment.

Each generation seems to forget the lessons learned from the past, the Sins of the Fathers.

We should be astutely aware that history keeps repeating itself negatively, time and time again because the common denominator in it, is the human factor and the consistency of predictability to how people in groups and large populations react to ideologies which threatens their Freedom and Liberty and individual profit and heritage.

Our history is the cornerstone of our future, and our history is being rewritten.

You shouldn't plan or look to the future until you first look at the past and understand its failures and successes.

I wish everyone had a "Quality" thinking mind.

It is actually a peaceful thinking mind and one that strives for Excellence.

The phrase, "Be all that you can be" is a Quality agenda.

It has all of the presence of building individual character towards the "Very Best of" expectations, which as we all know, is the topic of Quality and the outcome to the conclusion that

"Quality is Everything!"

WALSTON RULE #2

*"There are Exceptions to every rule,
but every rule is not the Exception"*

Quality has its humble beginnings at the personal (One-on-One) level.

With the skilled craftsman who has been trained and apprenticed through a vocational program and mentoring.

Who understands all of the physical aspects and properties of their craft and has experienced many levels of failures and recovery.

Someone, who has gone from a Journeyman Novice to Expert Master.

Like an engineer who has been educated in the respective science and mechanics of their discipline.

Who understands and develops the architectural and physical characteristics with anticipation of every aspect related to the design of what someone else will build.

Someone who has gone through the portal of imagination, through trial and error and has perfected a model or experiment for proven absoluteness.

Like a culinary artist who has years of preparing recipes and a multitude variety of cuisines.

Who understands the secrets of mixing compounds and substances of organic materials into tasteful and nutritious passions.

Someone who has gone from Cook to Chef.

With the soldier or law enforcer who has been extensively trained, self-disciplined, marksman and fighter, with a vision and determination.

Who understands the Rules of Engagement and winning the battles.

Someone so dedicated and focused, with the awesome authority of deadly force, that they would give their own life to preserve it.

In each of these vocations and countless others, the mastering of their skill set as a Top Performer is expeditiously achievable through applying what I refer to as the "Seven Quality Dedications".

1) Dedication to ones **Disciplined** Self
2) Dedication to ones **Principled** Self
3) Dedication to ones **Ethical** Self
4) Dedication to ones **Spiritual** Self
5) Dedication to ones **Learning** Self
6) Dedication to ones **Improving** Self
7) Dedication to ones **Achievement** Self

I would never say for example, "Do what I do" to someone unless I had an Expert skill set to lead as the example.

The old saying, "Never send a boy to do a man's job", has a lot of sound advice to it.

It's all about well-rounded education, training and experience, with a proven track record of successes.

So many times, Quality falls off by the wayside because of the incoherent ability to perform a function or task to its fullest extent due to lack of experience, training or vocational preparation.

I personally have found that "experience" adds more value to the performer than anything else.

Humankind has no instinctive characteristics born into our nature.

We are nothing like the other species within the animal kingdom on this planet.

We (humans) are the highest order of creation and were intended to have mastery and rule over the entire planet and all life-forms within it.

We learn everything we know and reason through a subjective mind everything we do. Even at that, you cannot properly apply what you've learned without hands-on, working experience.

All of our primeval actions as infants like crying because we are hungry or taking our beginning steps toward walking or babbling and talking, or anything else we believe we are evolving into are all just physical desires, needs and reactionary stimuli.

It requires us to be trained and schooled on everything we do in order to perfect our ability to perform in a Quality manner and succeed in our individual goals and aspirations.

We spend at a minimum, 12 years preparing between elementary through high school just to learn the basics so we can begin our adulthood on an even playing field with everyone else.

Our parents or guardians lend a big hand in the development of our attitudes about Quality through the traditional home setting we are subjected to.

How we are raised in the home setting determines how we learn and develop our true outlook of the Seven Quality Dedications mentioned earlier.

Do I apply what I've learned or what I've lived?

The well-balanced perspective to any situation is to call upon your experience as well as what you've learned, through educational training or trial and error.

Everything we do must coincide with our ability to apply action.

If we only absorb information and retain substance of knowledge, then we lack the practical means to exercise action and set Quality in motion.

It's all about **Application** and not **Substance**.

Action is the human kinetic energy releasing a plan or strategy and Substance is that stored energy waiting for an action to release it.

Substance leaves you sitting in a classroom or behind a desk, all bloated out and believing anything anyone tells you...like a mushroom, in *the dark and feeding on crap.*

Full of theories and metaphorical notions.

Application is what builds things!

It's what takes on the enemy and wins battles.

It's how we achieve what we plan to do.

Every strategy and well thought out plan are only a bunch of characters on paper or parchment, lost to obscurity, until the application of implementing it begins.

The best Quality in achieving success comes from the experience and leadership of executable succession and a proven track record of accomplishments.

In Ancient Times, with the building of great cities, structures and monuments, civilization was dependant on the individual talents of a skilled apprentice labour force under the guidance of Expert Masters, who dedicated their life's work to a single skill set discipline.

Out of this came vocational tradesmen who developed the art and craft of their expert talent, such as masons, stone cutters, bricklayers, carpenters, tool and weapons makers, blacksmiths, farmers, soldiers, etc.

These tradesmen implemented standard protocols, Tricks of the Trade (so-to-speak), which applied the basic physical and mechanical laws of nature and developed science.

In many instances, what they did was so unique that no one else could do it and was viewed as the magic of their art.

We marvel in modern times at how prehistoric people could build structures such as the great pyramids or the colossal lost cities of the ancient world, or monoliths like Stonehenge, the

Great Wall of China or the great stone images on Easter Island.

Notwithstanding, the hand craftsmanship and placement of these structures was to precise Quality tolerances, without the use of precision cutting tools, hydraulics, lifting cranes, steel reinforcement, concrete mortar or electricity.

These and many other structures have stood the test of time, through the calamities of natural disasters and we still see the majesty of their labour as a testimony to the Quality of their craftsmanship, engineering and genius.

The fundamental link between any aspiring society or civilization, past, present or future, is in the foundation and enforcement of their laws and civil regulations.

The same holds true for use of common symbols and language conventions, which express universally the mindset of its people and communities.

With the advent of the modern Industrial Age and the introduction of the Assembly-Line Process, handcrafted product quickly gave way to mass production and products being made at a lower cost.

Along with this came a new Control Process called *Inspection.*

This term implies suspicion of Quality by virtue of its applied function within the manufacturing process, which is to verify the correctness and compliance of product being built during the Work In-Process operations or after-the-fact before product is shipped.

With handcrafted items, the craftsman themselves assures every aspect of the Quality from inception to finished goods.

With the Assembly-Line, the finished item is an assemblage of many different parts by a multitude of different sources who produce each piece as required to make the sum of the whole finished goods.

The individual pieces could come from outside sources (Suppliers or Subcontractors) or internal departments within the parent assembly site.

In this scenario, the assurance of the product Build to Print aspects are determined by the interpretation of a drawing or instruction by individuals making the parts as required to the design characteristics.

The experience of knowing the part being manufactured is not as necessary as having the ability and skill set to read and interpret the media set before an operator or machinist building the part.

In order to give consistency for interpreting drawings and aiding in the inspection process, an array of industrial protocols had to be devised.

Design and development, drawing symbol conventions, manufacturability, inspection and many others needed to be standardized and agreed upon for global consideration.

From the 1950's through the 1980's the United States Department of Defense set the world's protocol standards with published rules and guidelines called Military Standards (Mil-Std) and Department of Defense Standards (DoD-Std).

Embedded within these were a set of protocols just for manufacturing assurance of Quality.

During this period, Quality was not seen as being synonymous within the company or business setting. It was seen as a cost burden, due to Inspection as being seen as a redundant process with no value-added benefit.

It had to become a separate entity, a required organization called QA (Quality Assurance), and had its own set of Mil-Stds such as the Mil-I Specifications (Inspection System Requirements) and the infamous Mil-Q-9858 (Quality Program Requirements)

Under these guidelines the QA Organization had two distinct departments:

1) **QC** (Quality Control)- A group of Inspectors (Hourly) who played COP and inspected the Quality into the product through Detection Methods and reporting non-conformances for corrective actions and most likely Rework (even Scrap), then resubmitting to Inspection for another round of Detection then finally Acceptance and Buy-Off.

   Within QC are a couple of sub-groups:

   • **Receiving Inspection**- Inspection of purchase order parts/material coming in from Out-Source Supplier/Vendors, or subcontractors.

   • **In-Process Inspection**- Inspection of parts/product within WIP (Work-In-Process) produced to internal Job/Work Orders, Travelers, Rework/Repair Orders.

   • **Final Inspection**- The last stage of the Inspection Cycle and last chance to find defects or anomalies before the product is given acceptance and routed to Stock or shipped for customer delivery.

2) **QE** (Quality Engineering)- A group of individuals (Salaried) whose training, education and experience bestowed the title of Engineer, because they could understand and contribute to the design aspects with Engineering of the manufactured product. In reality, these individuals were mostly non-degreed, hands-on types who came from specialized commodities and were embedded within the QA Organization to become a "Value Added" liaison resource with Design Engineering, Manufacturing Engineering, Production Assembly and the Government Auditing Representative.

As the escalation of the "Cold War" political machine intensified through the 1960's, the Department of Defense

(DoD) was being appropriated billions of dollars by the U.S. Congress for research and development on programs for our military arsenal.

Consequently, as these became production manufacturing contracts, hundreds of millions of dollars were being pumped into new private sector industries.

This rapidly grew and became known as the Aerospace Defense Industry.

Within this same timeframe, the race for space started and the National Aeronautics and Space Administration (NASA) was being developed.

With a different more stringent set of guidelines and standards than the DoD, NASA was going where no man had gone before, mandating Human Safety of Flight into space exploration.

This placed emphasis on Quality to the highest levels ever conceived.

Words like Fail-Safe, Quad-Redundancy, Phase-Gate, SPC, Six Sigma and Data Acquisition became new terms and methodologies.

Science and technology were beginning an upswing as never before seen in human history.

Since the discovery and usage of fire and the wheel, from Pre-Historic times to the Middle Ages, mankind didn't do much as far as transcending technology from using domestic animals and carted vehicles up to the late 19th Century A.D.

The biggest and lasting contribution through this time period had been the invention of Gun Powder and the Egg Noodle by the Chinese and in retro, the Seven Wonders of the Ancient World.

The Seven Wonders and Architectural Achievements of the Ancient World were just that, wonders how they ever got built.

It really is something to ponder on, when great achievements in Engineering and Mechanics came about by what were considered primitive people.

Nothing within the technology of these respective cultures had any other evidence which sparked the grandeur of these structured monuments.

Yet there was a common Quality of design engineering, architecture and mechanical building capability available through their citizenry.

Over many centuries, slow technological advancements in weapons and warfare armament were made through discovery of simple metal alloys and the usage of gun powder as a destructive substance.

The introduction of the gun and rifle made great strides in the science of mechanics to evolve man out of the Stone Age, chucking spears and shooting arrows to snatch their prey or kill their enemies.

Through all of this, Quality had been at the hand of the individual craftsman as passed on through apprenticeships and master tradesmen.

The first fifty years of the 20th Century saw more technological achievement in every area of science than all of the previous periods of human history combined.

With the invention of the electric light bulb and its commercialization, very quickly new industries began developing around more and more patents being issued for inventions using electricity and products mass produced for the general public.

New innovations, like the telephone, radio, motion pictures, phonograph, X-Ray machine; appliances like the refrigerator, dishwasher, washing machine, microwave oven, all came about within decades of each other.

Many of these transitioned from hand manual devices into automated running machines, with timer cycles, so the work was done leaving the individual free to do other things.

Never before had a single technology base revolutionized the entire world simultaneously.

With all of the innovations came considerations for safety, considering high voltage could kill you if not properly controlled and protected.

With safety, usually Quality follows as a means to police and enforce the manufacturing processes...and so it goes, that Quality was somehow integrated.

The real turning point into our present-day science and technology was replacing the vacuum tube with the invention of the transistor in 1955 and the introduction of semiconductors which birthed the Age of the Computer.

Solid State Electronics with thru-hole circuit card assemblies (large components) rapidly moved into micro-electronics (microscope size components) and surface mount wave solder techniques, as the developments of space age technologies transformed the electronics industry.

With the aerospace industries trying to keep up with these new innovations and their evolving technologies, the demand for smaller and smaller components to be sandwiched into smaller delivery and deployment packages, with weight reduction considerations, the processes and procedures needed to keep in line with the changing standards.

This would very quickly, within a few decades, skyrocket the entire world into the Information Age and totally transform communications and human interaction into a Global Community through an electronic, speed of light media called, the Internet.

The impact on Quality would be felt globally as well, with the need for solidarity and moving away from the U.S. DoD/Mil Standards, into an International Standards baseline.

We would see third world countries become main-stay nations in supplying both human and technology resources to the Industrial G3 superpowers, until they themselves would rank as a financial partnership and alliance with the superpowers.

The development of the ANS (American National Standards) and ISO (International Standardization Organization) standards ushered in the globalization for manufacturing goods and services.

The idea of such a thing has sinister roots.

To unite a standardized global community, especially from a European model, seemed like the political beginning of a One World Order, almost prophetic in proportion.

There were many of us within the management leadership of the Aerospace / Defense Industry that absolutely hated the idea of sacking the Mil-Std's for ANSI because of the underhanded association with incorporating a new International (Global) Standards base.

Even harder to swallow was ISO.

It appeared that the great and mighty U.S. Standards and the lead the United States had held for over four decades was disintegrating fast as the United Nations based EU and NATO finally had a triangular constituency in which to topple the U.S. dominance.

The U.S. had dictated and wrote the handbook receipt for production and assembly manufacturing and was being challenged by the liberal thinking commissions of the new European Union (EU).

As the EU started to absorb more and more countries into its consortium, they were actually considering calling themselves, the United States of Europe.

A bold and sarcastic idea, but not one the ultra liberal Germans, French and Italians wanted to actually embrace.

Besides, the real purpose behind the International Consortium was not to unite, but to build a Union of Global Dominance and Registrar enforcement.

ISO and the follow-on insurgency of AS / EN / JISQ 9000, 9100 and 9xxx are "Big" business and a huge bureaucracy of control.

The Registrar concept is a bunch of Third-Party auditors who impose exorbitant fees and mandatory audits to justify their existence.

It appealed immediately to the Elite and Nose-Thumbing Institutional Thinkers, Professor Types who never in their lives applied any Hands-On Application in Industry before.

Mostly Bank Auditors and Accountants who could implement exorbitant auditing models and gain control over a business infrastructure with dominant regulations and newly imposed Global Diversity (Laws).

The subjective manner of the audits appears to be towards helping your business become process streamlined and documenting every aspect of those processes.

In a nutshell, write down what you do (Procedures) and do what you're writing down (Processes). Kind of makes sense, a No Brainer…Right?

The problem becomes apparent when what you say you'll do has to be written around what They say you Must Do; and the policing of enforcement that is imposed along with it.

A whole new Gestapo style industry and career path was being born.

Once the auditing begins, it quickly becomes very business resource consuming, with the average day being a full eight hours and the average audit length being three days with a full out-briefing with all leadership management present, a mandatory requirement.

It could have been stopped just as the development was birthing as a throw back of the Big "Q" and Quality Circles turbulence in the 1980's, but like anything embraced by the Elite Class and the wizards of advanced learning institutions, it was enthralled and hailed as the next evolutionary step towards Total Quality Improvement.

The benchmark for it, of course, was the Aerospace/DoD Industry.

The QA discipline, procedural implementation and structured organization was already in place with the Mil-Std protocols.

In a sense, so was the auditing and management organization of the Defense Contract Administration (DCAS), who rode herd on all of the government defense contractors.

As the manufacturing industries moved away from the Mil-Std's to embrace ANSI and ISO, there were trade-offs as far as cost savings to implement and benefits of improved Quality through Total Quality Management Enterprising.

Another couple of new terms and annex organizations would come out of this called Mission Assurance, Performance Excellence and Enterprise...we'll talk about those later on.

As one version of ISO was being implemented, it seemed like a few years later another new version was being released and the Certificate Registrar was requiring it to be implemented, along with new audits, additional fees and expanded infrastructure (*deeper roots*).

Many companies and small businesses bellied-up due to the implementation costs of the required content sections, procedural infrastructure and consultant fees associated with obtaining their ISO Registrar, somewhat like the survival of the fittest.

Not to mention that on average it would take a company a year to impose the required infrastructure, procedures and manpower to gear up for the initial Registrar Audit to take place.

But when the big aerospace, aviation and government agencies finally bought into the ANS and ISO as the Mainstay of Institutionalized Quality, they demanded every company get on board and get certified in order to put you on their Approved Vendor List, then the choice was made for you.

That becomes the Catch-22 for so many businesses...either Do It or No Contract Awards. (*No business coming your way!*)

As time has shown, all of the Quality Improvement methodologies, corrective / preventative action measures and mandatory management involvement has been a wonderful thing in the big inter-departmental, multi-organizational, mega-program corporations and the government subsidized companies of the EU.

Considering how inherently wasteful they are with government funded taxpayer money and the cost associated with the human element and hundreds of thousands of dollars in defects, rework and scrap, any kind of structured organization with procedures, process improvements, Cost of Poor Quality, reduction of rejects and errors is going to automatically render a false sense of savings.

Like low hanging fruit on a tree, you can easily pick off the obviously easy issues and get instant results with successful trends.

New organizations, departments, career paths, Quality Institutes and Learning Centers, consultants, seminars, software and books have permeated every industry (Commercial, Private, Government) and sector of business.

A true Global Enterprise with billions of dollars, millions of participants' and hundreds of thousands of employees; and whatever new version of ISO/AS9100 there is, will be the most intrusive yet.

Is the time, investment and hassle of the Third-Party Audit Gestapo worth all the hype of your ISO?

Well, if you're Corporate America making hundreds of millions, even billions of dollars in profit, or your customers demand it in order for you to do business with them, or if the business leadership and management wants to be competitive with the competition down the street, or if you just like proudly hanging banners inside and outside the facility, then YES, it's all worth it.

On the other hand, if you're a Middle America Small Businessperson, relentlessly trying to make ends meet, or you can't seem to get ahead of your budget forecasts and overhead due to increased taxes, healthcare cost and intervention from the government bureaucracy, or maybe you're a Mom and Pop Shop with five employees and running a sweet little supplier business with a single commodity specialty with a nice customer base, or even a Special Process House and you have all of the certificates related to the Special Process you're performing, then the answer will be a big and resounding NO!

Personal Note: *Since the beginning of his career path, the author has been schooled, trained and literally dragged through the ISO/AS9100 mud in every way imaginable; with a total of seven companies in which the responsibility for implementing and maintaining the Quality System was mandatory. Three of these from the ground up to achieving full Registrar Certification and first audit passage. In my humble opinion, none of them were worth the time, effort and cost. It is a forced practice you learn to accept and in time try to demonstrate compliance when the Registrar Gestapo show up to audit you.*

The one thing ISO tries to overcome is hidden factors like tribal knowledge and verbal direction from within the organizational structure of a business, by documenting every process and action each organization performs and place them under the umbrella of a Quality System in which the Management Team is responsible for implementing and maintaining.

This attempt tries to mandate Quality as everyone's responsibility, with the perspective that Quality is synonymous throughout the business structure, but this is not empirical or pragmatic.

Believe me having an ISO/AS9100 Quality System in place does nothing to enforce that.

We still have the human factor to control and deal with before and after any institutional Quality System is put in place.

ISO imposes the structure and guidelines, with the policing activities of forced auditing and corrective actions; not the deep-down discipline and desire to want Quality.

When you get right down to the reality of why we need sets of standards in the first place, is because of the "Human Factor" and the mass production of product in an assembly-line environment with influx of skill set diversity and the typical "Turn-Around" of human resources being introduced into the Assembly Process. You need written procedures to processes, so anyone can be trained to the exact way product has been designed to be built or services have been designated to functionally work.

Unlike times past, with the individual craftsman who dedicated their entire adult career path towards a single skill set and cultural setting, the Industrial Age, with its assembly-line mass produced products, you can have unskilled and partially trained individuals working in areas of industries that they did not apprentice in or dedicate their life's work to.

People coming in off the street, who just needed a job and can be trained, OJT (On-the-Job Training), in order to perform a single or multiple function task.

It all comes down to the Human Element.

That's where the true emphasis lies and the bottom-line to believing that,

"Quality is Everything!"

WALSTON RULE #3

"Quality is what separates a Good company,
from a Great company"

"Scotty, Beam Me Up", became one of the most iconic phrases of the last portion of the 20th century.

A line used on the T.V. series from the mid to late 1960s, "Star Trek", by the infamous character of Captain James T. Kirk of the Starship USS Enterprise.

It is still used to this day as an adage meaning, "Please get me the hell out of here."

I wonder how many people use that or feel it relates to the jobs they have or places they work at.

Two Polls conducted in 2018 and again in 2023 estimates that sixty percent of the U.S. working class are either unhappy with their jobs and career path or with the employers they work for.

Contrary to how most of the media and opposing political factions have portrayed our economics during the last decade, as being the worst since the 1930's Great Depression, the comparison is not similar in mindset or situation at all.

In contrast to the 1930's, seventy-five percent of the people who had jobs were feeling blessed in just having a job and thanking God for it!

There was no unemployment insurance; you either worked or starved.

The wages associated with almost every job dropped dramatically in proportion to the oppressed situation of the national economy.

I remember my grandfather, who during this time period was in his early 40's, telling me stories about how you'd work all day (12 hours) for fifty cents and that a really good wage for a day's labour was one dollar. A loaf of bread was a penny, butter was two cents and a chicken for the pot was thirty-five cents.

You didn't think about Quality, it was a given.

What ever a man did, he did to the best of his ability, with what he was given to do it with.

The unemployment between the 1930's and now is not comparable either.

At the height of the Great Depression, between 1932-33, the national unemployment rate hovered around 25%.

During the 2008-2009 economic crisis the national unemployment rate was hovering around 9.5%.

It's the same as it was when Ronald Reagan inherited the worst economy and recession since the Great Depression of the 1930's by the Carter Administration, as he came into office in 1981, and the highest unemployment rate inherited by the Trump Administration in 2025 from the Biden Administration of 7.1%

All the hype and comparisons that were being associated to the 2008 fiasco as the worst National Depression since the 1930s, was all political staging and used as fear monger tactics to bring this nation under submission towards a socialistic agenda...NOT GOOD FOR AMERICA!

Reagan was able to make substantial growth in the economy by keeping the government out and putting the private sector in the driving seat through good old Capitalism, and Trump by imposing International Tariffs and making trade deals around that threat to our advantage.

President Reagan so honestly summed it up by stating, "The problem isn't with government; the problem **is government!**"

By the end of his second term, Reaganomics pro-growth economic policies paid off tremendously and over 18 million jobs were created between 1983-89 and the unemployment rate had leveled out at 5.2%.

Reagan did it by lowering taxes in the right areas to expand the private sector growth and with investment in DoD/Aerospace technology growth.

The Obama Administration almost brought us to our knees by increasing taxes and lowering our GDP down to 1.3% by the end of his 2nd Term in Office.

The ONLY reason the United States did not go into a full blown 1930's type of depression is because we bought our way out of the banking meltdown.

We avoided another 1929 "Run on the Bank" type of "Crash" scenario because George Bush began a payout of Billions of Taxpayer Dollars in order to stop that from happening.

Barack Obama added a few more Trillions to the Deficit, but like a kid in a candy shop he couldn't seem to stop spending our money.

We poured so much bailout money into the banking institutions, they couldn't fail.

The wizards in the Bush and Obama Administration would not allow our Capitalistic structure to work and the normal and healthy attrition of failed businesses and banks who made bad management and financial decisions, to go bankrupt.

Instead, the government either bailed them out or bought them up with taxpayer money.

I think that we saw a very negative paradigm shift with the Obama Administration's policies (or lack of), to not encourage the private sector enterprises to gain more business advantage by lowering taxes and give immediate incentives for loans and relief in Health Care costs.

At that time, the only thing we had going for us was foreign governments buying into our debt. As long as other nations were willing to buy-up our national debt in order to own their land share of the United States of America and we keep the Treasury supplied with newly printed cash, then we're still in business.

President Trump gave us an administration that looked at curbing our Trade Deficit with China and the EU and the

World, cutting taxes to historic record Lows (with the Great New Deal) and reducing our foreign spending to secure other government military, NATO being the big one and evening out our 37+ Trillion Dollar National Deficit.

It's so ironic, I was talking with some colleagues at a Quality Conference in Fresno, California about this subject and how each of us remembered the "Glory Days" (or in some people's vocabulary- "The Good Old Days") of the Aerospace / Defense Cold War Era.

Cost Plus Contracts, virtually unlimited resources in new technologies, especially in exploratory sciences and no end to well-paying jobs.

Our problem from the 1960's through the end of the 80's was that we were raised by spending money and lots of it.

I'm part of the generation that was raised in this, the "Baby Boomers", the children of the "Greatest Generation", which goes back to the post WWII sudden expanse (Boom) in population between 1948-1963.

The great upsurge in technology and research was introduced in the early 1960's, when President Kennedy announced the United States' dominance in putting a man on the moon before the decade ended.

Behind the scenes was this little nation, which with the help of their previous enemy (the United States), was crawling out of the ashes of their own destructive desires to rule the world through military force.

Japan was the first to come out of the stereotype of being a post-war beaten, island nation, to embracing the Total Quality Management concepts of Dr. W. Edwards Deming.

They would transform their society into robotons, who would dedicate all of their efforts into one national mindset.

The attention was shifted from Military dominance towards Industrial dominance and universal thinking.

All effort was focused towards a single Quality mindset and implemented philosophy for national education and training;

from elementary school children to every worker in every industry.

This was a come up from behind (slap-in-the-face) to the great and mighty industrial power of the United States.

It was our own fault for disavowing such revolutionary ideas when Dr. Deming tried to introduce Quality Improvement techniques to the Big U.S. Automotive Car Manufactures and was either laughed at or told to go somewhere else.

So, he did, and the Japanese not only understood the importance of his concepts and teaching, but corner-stoned their dominance in the automotive world through embracing it.

LOL…just look at the sick shape the Detroit Automakers are in since the 2009 Financial Crisis continuing into the 2020 COVID-19 Pandemic fiasco.

In 2009 Chrysler once again, twice within thirty years, had their hands out for government bailout monies so they wouldn't go bankrupt, along with General Motors and their conglomerations.

Even though we, the American Taxpayers, were the ones to actually bail these bastards out of financial ruin, we are not seeing any real change in their bad habits.

Oh yeah, the new GM cars pair the EU Automakers and the Japanese as far as copying body styles and options, but as far as Quality, the USA is still behind the Eight-Ball in this industry.

It is still the same old graft with the unions, politicians and special interests.

It's all about that *quick at hand* magic they are so good at with the advertisement propaganda and the forecast of devastation for the whole nation if they don't get the billions to maintain their wasteful union infrastructure, unbelievable profit margins and executive bonus structure.

All except one were in line for the government taxpayer bailout monies in the 2009 fiasco and that exception was Ford Motors.

Ford embraced a real Quality Improvement and Campaign Program early on in the 1980's, while the other Fat Cats in Detroit were busy doing *quid pro quo* and making sure they had their congressional constituents in line.

Ford saw the light as being one of the big automakers who could not compete with the Japanese without embracing a true and robust overhaul of their Quality System and Assembly Processes.

The design of their cars and the impact of how Quality would be implemented in every department, with every employee and all aspect of their products, was viewed as the most critical criteria.

They realized that a day of reckoning and redemption was coming sooner or later.

Even in the 2009 meltdown crisis, Ford's Quality foresight gave them the advantage in not needing government bailout monies and could once again be hailed as the "Come Back Kid" with the biggest bite in the market share pie.

Deming's 14 points to Quality Improvement revolutionized the Japanese industries.

It brought about the inspiration for Kaizen (Improvement) and the LEAN Process and eventually, the Toyota Production System (TPS), which was finally hailed as the greatest Improvement Model devised in modern history.

Even though Dr. Deming was the pioneer and the recognized individual source of bringing awareness to the Japanese manufacturing elite on how to improve their manufacturing processes through management intervention, there are a few others who rode on the coat-tails and inspiration of his work and message.

One in particular and worth mentioning is Masaaki Imai.

Mr. Imai in his own rite is regarded as the "LEAN Guru" and through his work in this area has a following which proclaims him as the Father of Continuous Improvement.

Deming of course, was thirty-five years on the Japanese scene preaching the message of Continuous Improvement with his 14 Principles for Management and the Seven Deadly Diseases before Masaaki Imai introduced his Lean Concepts.

Nevertheless, Mr. Imai has made a tremendous contribution to that arena as well.

In 1985 he founded the KAIZEN Institute in Switzerland and introduced a totally new concept the following year, through a book he published called *KAIZEN (KY'ZEN) The Key to Japan's Competitive Success.*

Kaizen means *Improvement* and the strategy of Kaizen calls for *never-ending efforts for improvement*, involving everyone in the organization, managers and workers alike.

It was the first book to introduce the concept and philosophy of "LEAN".

If you wanted to define what the intent of "LEAN" is, I've concluded that it is- *a production practice that considers the expenditure of resources for any goal other than the creation of value for the end customer to be wasteful and thus a target for elimination.*

Basically, LEAN is centered on preserving value with less work and LEAN manufacturing is a variation on the theme of efficiency based on optimizing flow.

No matter how hard the U.S. Automakers or the U.S. Manufacturing Industrial Corporations tried, the concepts that the Japanese were implementing and having great success with were being totally ignored.

The difference is how the Japanese were concentrating with improvement orientation through Process Thinking verse the Results Thinking application.

The Kaizen methodology concentrates at improving the process, rather than achieving certain results.

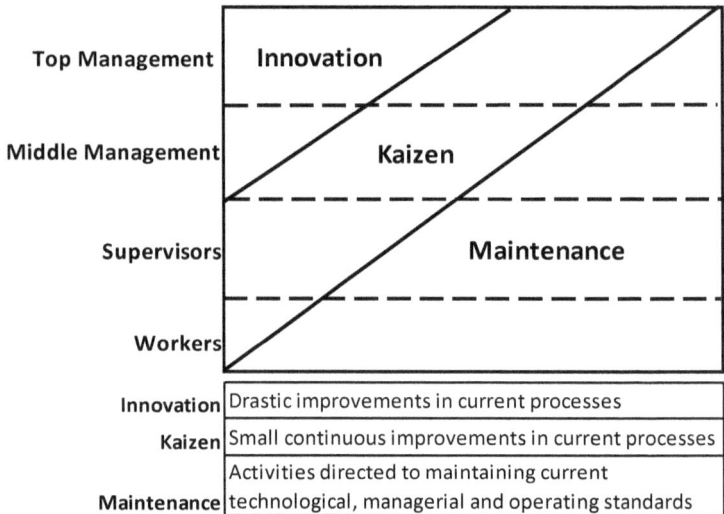

Innovation	Drastic improvements in current processes
Kaizen	Small continuous improvements in current processes
Maintenance	Activities directed to maintaining current technological, managerial and operating standards

Figure 3-1 Kaizen - Job Functions as perceived by
Japanese Managers

However, the success of the Japanese to implement any model of improved management practice or Continuous Improvement, in and of itself, was due to their strict cultural environment and submissive characteristics of the general population, "to submit to", a standard discipline and acceptance at a national level.

This is a matter of National Pride and duty and is more relevant in Asian cultures than with the Western World Populous.

In order to subdue this myth with western society, the new portrayal Asia would like us to believe is that their success is not based on any cultural disciplines or dictated national practices.

Masaaki Imai stated it himself when he wrote, *"Japanese management practices succeed simply because they are good management practices. This success has little to do with cultural factors. And the lack of cultural bias means that these practices can be – and are – just as successfully employed elsewhere."*

None of what Masaaki stated is true for the United States, as they only apply to the Japanese cultural and dominate disciplined or Imperialistic led societies.

The United States is a Freelance Society; Entrepreneur oriented and has no central governance control by disciplined dogma and distinct heritage or uniform cultural boundaries.

We are a melting pot of mixed races and cultural diversity and because of this, as our society accepts more and more liberal ideologies and introductions to shared global politics and enterprising, then the United States becomes less and less of a world dominance and leader of Free Enterprising.

Asia made an all-out attempt to dominate the U.S. Manufacturing Corporate structure during the 1980's and 90's, right here on American soil.

We entered 1981 with the worst economic depression and recession since the 1930's in America.

All bets were off with Wall Street and any loyalty to upholding American owned businesses or American Style infrastructure…who ever has the money, wins our loyalty.

As businesses started failing, unemployment started rising and property started getting cheap, the cry from Corporate America was "Sell! Sell! Sell!"

And SELL we did! as the big Flag Ships from Asia started coming on shore; Sony, Toyota, Nissan, MCA, Tyco, Kyocera, Mitsubishi and countless others began buying up land, corporations and building cultural infrastructures in the American Heartland.

With them came new job opportunities for the unemployed Americans, but also came Asian customs, business ethics and philosophies that were required to be embraced and practiced by all employees.

The new Asian Parent Corporations sent their management to run the American subsidiaries according to their leadership protocol and customs.

They wanted to make sure that none of the nasty and wasteful American habits infiltrated their streamlined and disciplined management protocols or young executives from the Homeland.

It was always immediately noticeable when one of our American Corporations was being assimilated by the Japanese:

1) The outward appearance of the company changed
   with better housekeeping.
2) Discipline in dress and edict were immediately
   introduced.
3) The parking lot seemed neater, and the cars parked
   in a more organized manner.
4) The Kaizen approach was being incorporated.

You would see all of the employees in the parking lot early in the morning, in some formation, doing exercising or calisthenics.

It was the Japanese belief that this would motivate or stimulate the mind to thinking process better, if the body was in better physical condition before you started work; and the Japanese had a distinct opinion about the over-weight, lazy American Worker.

But the biggest noticeable difference was the lack of any unions and the requirement (or Policy) not to allow any to form.

This is where I believe their biggest success manifested and paired the Japanese way of life, so that the discipline of management could run the business unaltered by unwanted or ruling outside forces.

The majority of opinions regarding the backward trends in U.S. built products, as being costlier and of lesser or inferior Quality to the Japanese over the last forty years, was being targeted towards the U.S. Organized Labour Unions.

The biggest deterrents with the Labour Unions was limiting worker task assignments and ability to expand beyond a job title description and the stranglehold with contract negotiations and striking (union workforce walking off the job to meet their demands).

The hold a union representative (Union Steward) has is beyond constructive for the Leadership and Management Team to affectively run the business, when bombardments of union grievances are being issued due to union employees not wanting to do certain functions which non-union employees or management (salaried employees) perform, which a union employee could do.

It could be something as simple as carrying a box of office supplies from one office to another.

Cross-training among workers in shared tasks is discouraged if not strictly forbidden.

The mindset doesn't match a Collective Teamwork environment where you can increase the "Value Added" resource capabilities of the business, but rather it supports the Unions Collective Bargaining posture and position which supports their agenda to politically control the business outside of the Management leadership.

The dangerous position that the corporate management leadership allows, is when a Union can infiltrate the workforce and have a say-so in the business management affairs.

The true mindset of the Union IS NOT to work with "Management", but to keep Management under Check; this way the Union postures their workforce members as "The Victims".

The victim image has enormous empowerment for the individual and influence with Federal and State laws and regulations, determining such things as discrimination, harassment, or wrongful termination.

Each mitigation of a grievance cuts into cost and time spent on non-job related and unnecessary work tasks.

The unions have imposed a political and legal infrastructure that businesses cannot afford or work affectively towards a Quality Centric Organization.

Unions impose a great deal of non-working idle time and an inherent, "It's not my job man" workplace mentality.

The other stifling affect of a union in business is the increased hourly worker rates and benefits compared to non-union workers in similar industries doing the same tasks or job classifications.

There is also the burden cost of union dues to the employees and the share of payment towards retirement funds that both employees and the corporate business shares in.

All of this takes a lot of money and personnel to support and manage, which is not incurred with a non-union business.

More and more, U.S. businesses are demanding a non-union shop in order to be competitive in the global market share.

It wasn't until the late 1980's into the early 1990's that the DoD / Aerospace contractors were embracing something called Big "Q".

The Big "Q" concept was an expression that contrasts the difference between striving for Quality in all of the business products and processes verses striving for quality in a limited or specific area, which was referred to as the Little "q".

Once the Federal government found out that Quality, and in particular the QA organization, could play a significant role in reducing Scrap and Rework Cost through better process controls, they got on board with implementing stronger Quality requirements in the contracts they were awarding.

The only problem with the American way of doing this, is the need to express ourselves through convoluted, lengthy and complex formulas, overly expressed theories and textbook training seminars and certification programs.

No one can understand how to implement programs or processes that are written like a college physics book or software programmers manual, with hundreds and thousands of pages in content unless a PhD from the Quality Institute of La-De-Da comes in as a consultant, at $100+ an hour and explains it.

In every situation it's like reading and interpreting the Bible, open to self-interpretations and self-expressions based on the individual's practical life experiences or desires to use the information for their own self edifications...this I'm calling and referring to as, "STB-OTP (Saturate the Brain-Overwhelm the Person)".

Riding on the Deming coattails were a few other Institutes of Higher Quality Improvement and Learning, with catchy phrase names which get the attention of impressionable (Wanna-Be) Quality Experts; all with a different perspective, model or approach to Quality Improvement.

Each offer courses and seminars, books, training materials and offer training experts to teach their dogma...it's an expensive business enterprise, one which the corporate mindset has made mandatory.

At the end, the recipient goes back to their business propagated, educated, certificated, and most likely constipated with theories, models and ideas which have no practical applications in their immediate business environment.

In this scenario, what's usually missing is the due diligence investigation and complete understanding on the part of the Leadership Management, to suffer the subjective consequences, proactive benefits, or negative impact that a new Quality application may have on their business.

The biggest aspects to be considered are added cost and additional resources (both human and facility) in order to implement and maintain the new Quality infrastructure needed to support the so called "Quality Improvement Program".

It's never as simple as just sending a few Key People who will lead the Quality Improvement Program.

They have to learn the techniques and applications of the new Improvement Model (Train the Trainer), get certified with all the manuals, other instruction paperwork and learning aids, then come back and implement, and it all takes off from there.

It's too broad and complex to be that simple and as such, the full scale and extent of its application and implementation is never revealed by the Institute Business Promoters.

Nevertheless, they are waiting on that call for HELP, when after you've figured out that it can not be a self implemented thing, to offer the long list of agenda and consulting resources that must be used in order for you to either get that Registrar Certificate or Lean / Quality Improvement Program and Processes up to fruition.

The implication of the Continuous Improvement Concept concedes that *everything is part of a process, and all processes can be improved*; but the application of this concept can be skewed and misrepresented by not including the most important aspect that:

"Quality is Everything!"

WALSTON RULE #4

"The guilty are always innocent,
just ask them"

The Optimist

Views that, intrinsically humankind (All People) want to do "good" and postulate themselves towards continuous self-improvement. That people evolve into higher intellect. They want to embrace virtues which set forth standards ensuring the Highest Quality possible. No one intentionally does a bad job or intentionally produces something of poor Quality. *"To Err is Human!"* Things will always get better! "Strength through Peace"

The Pessimist

Views that, no one has instinctive goodness. *"To Err is Laziness and a Lack of Self-Discipline!"* Everything is questionable due to our built in Human Error Factor. That people will cut corners and do work-rounds if it saves money, and no one catches them. If the glass isn't full, then it's half empty and moving towards the bottom unless action is taken to rectify the situation. The assurance of Quality is something that must be enforced daily. Things could get a lot worse. "Peace through Strength"

It could be said that the Optimist views life through "Rose Colored" glasses (a liberal thinker), where the Pessimist sees it with 20/20 vision and a sense of reality (a conservative thinker).

The truth is, both are the extreme of the other and both are needed in order to give a healthy balanced perspective of life's view.

I am one of those Quality Professionals that most of the time will sway towards the conservative perspective when making decisions and creating a center point of view.

Most Post-Neanderthal, endothermic creatures who walk upright on two legs, sees Quality as an important factor in gauging the essence of their life.

Anyone who doesn't is still a Knuckle-Crawler.

In my life's journey, I've found that a lot of emphasis is placed on the Quality of Life by most people.

Since the 1980's, the measures to base the Quality of Life in America has changed significantly.

One factor of this change has been the shift from a Single-Family Dwelling to Multi-Family Dwellings within the inner-city and metro areas of our country.

This has had a great impact to the infrastructure of city planning, utilities, and property values, as well as taking of the National Census.

It is also a shift from the established Americana "Nuclear Family", where you have a mother, father and off springs living in a single dwelling.

What's become way too familiar is an established ethnic tribal arrangement, where multi-families or relatives live within the same Single-Family dwelling.

In most instances, it is the moving in of immigrant offshore family members as refugee aliens or illegal members, housing with a Green Card or Work Visa resident who is here legally.

This harbors what I call "The Hidden Society" and legitimizes the growing illegal population; and with the onset of Sanctuary Cities and even States, the Hidden Society grows more out-of-control and unidentified. It also lends itself to illegal voting in our election process and issuance of state and federal benefits to these non-citizens, thus adding an extra burden to the legitimate tax paying citizens.

The contributing incomes of these outside members is not declared but used to support the overall residence.

This skews the dynamic of a neighborhood and definitely gives a false image of the demographics and impacts the property value of the immediate areas affected and more importantly, the infrastructure of resources (Water, Sewer, Energy, etc.) which the area was not originally designed for and has not been updated to include.

Another debacle for the Quality of Life in America is living "Beyond Your Means" lifestyles.

This is gauged by the consumption and gathering of material wealth that can be acquired in a relatively short period of time and sustaining it as long as possible.

No one living like this really sees a future in what they are doing.

The philosophy has been around as long as man...*Eat, Drink and be Merry, for tomorrow we shall die.*

Hence, human history has proven beyond doubt that mankind is instinctively self-serving.

We tend to be inherently cautious of outsiders coming into our family circles or cultural boundaries.

We begin with self, embrace self and end with self.

A Cultural Society depends on Group Consensus and a shared Common Lifestyle without outside intervention or diversity; they become "One People". Hence, the United States is not a Cultural Society, but a mixture of diversity and opposing ideologies (both Political and Social) and native lifestyles, which never assimilate into a Common Culture.

The main issue facing the United States continuing as a nation of "We the People" is not Immigration, but rather Assimilation.

Any voluntary action to share or embrace the needs of another is a learned process...and if I may say for a lot of us, a very painful learned process.

Taking ownership and responsibility for one's, own actions and mistakes is another Learned Process.

If Quality is the outcome in any way, shape, or form in all of this, then it is by coincidence, because Quality is the result of perfecting what we learn and skillfully applying it with consistency through our daily life.

There has to be a balance in life in order to achieve and sustaining health, happiness and the pursuit thereof.

I left out what most people would consider a pinnacle of achievement, "Wealth".

The reason for the exclusion is because Wealth for the majority of us is fleeting at best and has nothing whatsoever to do with health and happiness.

If I was to say, that obtaining these kinds of things is the direct result of my own efforts, then I am not only limiting my ability to achieve, but the ability to sustain any achievement.

The perception in the minds of most people is that the term Quality equates to achieving Perfection.

It's the label given to the highest attempt and outcome regarding skill, craftsmanship and having followed the design to manufacturing requirements if you're producing a product.

If you want to raise the confidence level of what you produce, you do that to a Quality Standard and set the outcome to a Higher Quality Level (HQL).

The opposite is what you'll find at the five and dime discount stores.

In every instance where I've seen the hype given to promoting Quality in the business setting, it usually comes about because there is no real way to promote Quality from within.

Either the management commitment is not there, or management isn't running the business.

Other insurrections like improper or lack of training, bad process procedures, a tribal legacy mentality and very loose discipline are prevalent and help to dissolve a Quality setting.

All in all, it equates to either a non-existent or very poorly organized Quality (QA) Group.

One sure-fire way most businesses approach improving their Quality is through a Quality Awareness Program, kind of like a campaign drive.

It starts with a theme, like…" We love Quality" or "Quality is Everyone's Responsibility" or "Quality starts with YOU!"

These should only be awareness campaigns, but much too often become the entire effort to promote Quality and a misguided agenda, which usually falls off after a month or so.

It's much easier in the minds of the passive thinkers to organize and push an agenda (*make a show of it, a fundraiser approach*), than to implement processes and procedures.

You need to build the infrastructure of Quality into each functional organization and train everyone (Top→Down), to activate and maintain their portion of responsibility and overall awareness to Quality…and oh yeah, there must be repercussions for not doing that.

Quality must become synonymous throughout the business and the main theme to achieve that is, "Quality is Everything!"

The deception is making it look like everyone is behind the Quality campaign approach by using One-Liners, then it is to enforce a Quality Program within the functional organizations of the business.

That approach takes management commitment to change.

The change has to come from within in order to appear from without.

The typical misrepresentation of a business approach to a Total Quality Program, is by promoting the One-Liners in Staff Meetings or All Hands Meetings like, "we need to keep a Quality Mindset", or "Quality is everybody's job".

Another is to display banners like "Quality is America Made" hanging all over the facility even with an American Flag above, below, or right next to it, like there's a patriotic credibility to the Quality Campaign.

Some businesses go the extra mile by publishing a Quality Thought for the Week via company email, thinking this promotes a uniform solidarity and Team environment.

Nothing could be further from the truth.

You eventually become numb to the lifeless phrases because there's no action behind it.

It supposedly demonstrates the outward appearance that *We're Serious about Quality,* when in reality it has a negative effect on the general population and constituents within the business who are told one thing yet do another.

In rare instances, like with the Ford Motor Company, they started a Total Quality Program from within, starting with a total management commitment to change the culture and infrastructure with strict Quality Guidelines.

Then the campaign was developed to push the management commitment that "Quality is Job One" and Ford became the success story and a Primary Quality Model for the American Automotive Industry.

A true Quality Program that is properly implemented starts from the Top→Down, with upper management through the ranks below and to every worker, embracing and dictating the policies and agenda.

There must also be a discipline that imposes repercussions if non-compliances are identified.

These follow-thru as corrective actions and due diligence for the verification of non-recurrence and making sure the problem resolution gets to the root cause and has a closed-loop fix.

It needs to be robust enough to include personnel sanctions such as disciplinary actions and even termination for repeat offenders.

Just a footnote: The author has yet to see in his career as a Quality Professional any company step up to the plate and declare or say that "Quality is Everything!" In my humble yet bold opinion, the bottom-line is that companies are in business to make money and when that ability to make money is hindered or slowed, then Quality takes a backseat to profits no matter what they proclaim.

Let's look at some misperceptions given by promotional One-Liners:

- **_Let's give our customer(s) what they want..." A Quality Product"._**

  The "Customer" is just like any other consumer, they want the best product, with the highest Quality possible, for the cheapest price and of course, delivered on-time or immediately available. So, as the customer, that sounds like a reasonable yet demanding request. Nevertheless, this phrase has to be a constant thing being drilled into the minds of the worker/employee and repeated time and time again throughout the manufacturing industries. If Quality really was everything to everyone (first on their minds), then the campaign message would be inherent by their actions, their work protocol and ethics. Thinking about Quality and being Quality, are very different aspects of a person's philosophy and habit. It's like Matter and Anti-matter.

- **_Let's put forth 100% effort and obtain 100% Quality._**

  No one has ever seen Quality success by working harder or putting in longer hours or working six/seven days a week. There's a "Burnout" factor to be considered and the downward curve of productivity due to fatigue and increased mistakes.

  When business management concedes to working extended shifts and long hours for individuals as a practice to compensate for backlogs or over bookings of deliveries, then this is a proven doomed practice and leads to eventual failure.

  Working to a set plan and having well documented procedures and work instructions with each person trained and disciplined, gives much higher success rate towards

Quality. What if the 100% effort is expended towards building the product wrong or with inherent design flaws or mistakes due to a floor culture of legacy and tribal knowledge mentality, which works to undocumented protocols. Then the product is already less than 100% Quality and the effort and cost moves beyond what was planned and budget forecasted and the effort becomes 110%->120%->150% of the expected forecast. Rework and overtime must be imposed and mostly procurement of more parts/material to replace what is being scrapped through the MRB process adds to the Cost of Poor Quality tally.

- *"Quality is what we're all about".*

What Quality is really all about is compliance and setting your goal towards perfection. What we're all about is sometimes something else. No matter how hard we try, as humans we have a built-in defect rate, we make mistakes. Some studies suggest as much as 5% on average per task performed, so that equates to a less than 100% Quality rating for each and every one of us. To be all about Quality means unbelievable discipline and self-determination towards weighing each situation one encounters against the standard of Quality established for the individual at the workplace or personal life setting. Interact with each situation or task as an auditor would, against a mental checklist of absolute "Must Do's". Then give evaluation to the things not compliant and follow-up with corrective and preventative actions. Take the time to then close the error loop with verification of non-recurrence so there is a permanent fix always implemented. Paradigm shift from **Detection** (finding errors made after-the-fact) to→ **Prevention** (correcting errors being made as they happen), with the goal emphasis on Total Quality Improvement.

- *The "Team" ensures Success…there's no "I" in Team!*

The first big misconception of the "Team" concept is hailing it as the catalyst which makes improvements happen. The second is that the consensus of the "Team", foregoes the individual dictation or decision of an expert. The third is that the "Team" should be made up of many experts, rounding off the consensus to One Opinion, like One Mind with One Outcome. In many instances, more than not, the multiple opinions of the team membership stalemate with no decision and no outcome. There better be an "I" at the workplace! The "I" in "Team" is me doing my job according to the skills and experience I was hired to perform and taking full responsibility for the job I am performing. That includes making decisions for my area of responsibility which are not challenged or circumvented. The most successful Teams are the groups of individuals assigned to a project, where the individual members act as respective functional experts of their skill set and commodity and as a collective group, they achieve their planned goal. The bottom-line is if you don't all work together to resolve issues and move past the in-fighting amongst the functional organizations, then you're dead in the water. This is true in any business and any situation where two or more people are working together. However, the "Team" scenario does not in and of itself guarantee success and should not be used as the leadership model to run the business at the functional organizational level. It is best used at the Project Level.

- *"We'll accept nothing less than 100% Quality".*

    Another phrase that is used like a sales pitch which will get you in trouble with your customers and your reputation, if for some unknown or unseen reason you have a recall or issue a service bulletin because of bad product or service. This banner comes down really quick if that happens. There's no need to proclaim to the world that you'll accept nothing less than 100% Quality. That should be part of your business strategy and Quality Policy. It surely is implied if your business is an ISO type Registrar. The brazen boldness of proclaiming such a statement makes most Quality Professionals feel like a used car salesman. Face it, life is all about compromises, just as Quality achievements are, due to the human element and the non-conformance factor. This is exactly why every business who wants to achieve success with Quality, imposes a Quality Program which implements Continuous Improvements into their processes and built-in protocol.

It would consistently be in the best interest of every person and any business if one over-riding perspective and perception was imposed; this being the demand for Quality to be so high, that nothing else is acceptable.

If you really wanted to shout something from the rooftop which best supports that philosophy, then it would be:

"Quality is Everything!"

WALSTON RULE #5

*"Success is what you achieve when you're
building a Legacy,
Legacy is what you leave when you've been successful"*

Let's spend some serious conversation on Quality Assurance (QA), which is something near and dear to my heart.

The organization of QA is important for any business to have within their infrastructure.

However, having a QA Department does not, in and of itself, assures that a business is producing, servicing, or delivering anything of Quality, nor does holding a Third-Party Registrar like ISO or AS9100.

There is no Quality "Mystique" in any QA organization or Quality System.

It's not like someone orders "release the hounds!" and the QA dogs are out chasing down the bad product and fixing all of the Quality violations.

I'd be in favor of relabeling Quality Assurance as "Business Compliance" (BC).

There is no actual assurance of Quality, only Verification of Compliance.

Remember, Quality is- *the measurement of performance against a standard, to the degree of excellence which qualifies the outcome of any given function or process by which something is produced or created.*

Therefore, the Quality of anything is subjective to the End-User, even if the verification of compliance is 100%, the Quality could be unacceptable to the End-User.

The assurance for Quality should be the requirement assigned and designated to each and every individual within a business and the motto "Quality is Everything!" on the lips of every person.

It should be the guarantee of their Producible Output and the measure of their Value-Added Resource, as well as the metric for evaluating their Performance and judging their Merit.

The QA organization should only be a compliance verification activity and a minimum Inspection effort at that.

The worst mindset anyone can have is to add more Inspection to any process.

Hiring more QC Inspectors is a Regressive posture and leads to handholding of the individuals who are performing the functional tasks.

QA becomes a crutch at that point in supporting inadequate skill sets and maintaining a lower intellect of the persons performing the functional operation tasks.

The QA Management Policy should never allow for QC to do spot checking or courtesy inspections (1st piece look-sees), from the production assembly / operations work centers.

The model point that pushes the paradigm from Detection (needing increased Inspection to catch defects) towards Prevention (fixing the problem at the root cause) is 1st Pass Yield and identifying the "Hidden Factory" for Cost of Poor Quality (Rework, Scrap and Warranty).

Don't get me wrong here, Key Verification Points within any process are required and should be a third party independent of the organization building a product or performing a service.

1st Pass Yield is defined under Inspection and Test Points within the Instructional Paperwork (WIP Traveler/Shop Order Operation Sequences) of the Production Build.

Each process should have a functional flow outlined, with every *Node* within the entire process mapped as to performing operations and 1st Pass Inspection Points.

A successful tool that QA would impose within the Functional Flow would be labeled as **P**rocess **Q**uality **I**ndicators (PQI).

Each PQI is a potential 1st Pass Yield and Key Verification Point (KVP) for inspections or testing, to assure the requirements of the product design or specifications have been fulfilled.

These are plotted as such to gather yield data which can identify improved Process Controls at the various Operations in the Product Build Sequence.

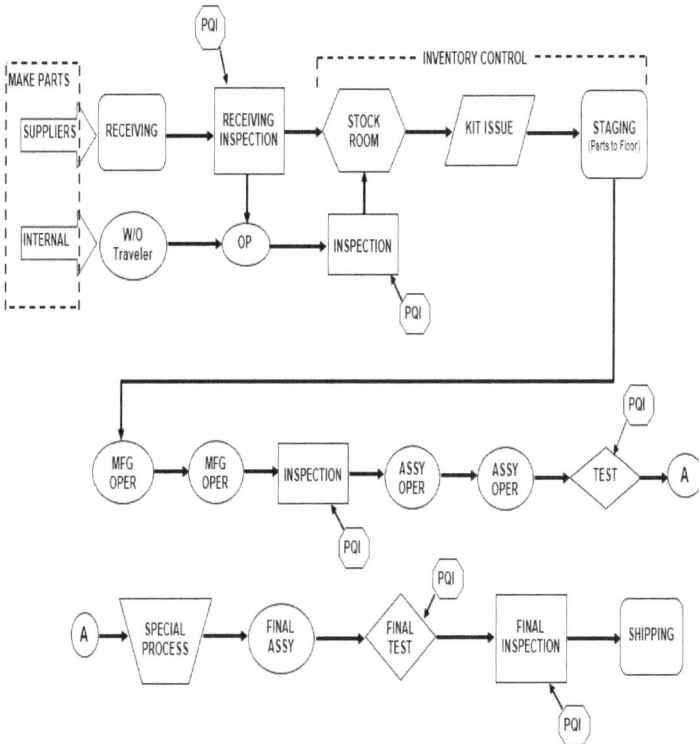

Figure 5-1 Production Manufacturing Functional Flow
with PQI's

By Definition:

Product Quality Indicators are points within a manufacturing process flow where data is gathered for monitoring product non-conformances and eventual corrective actions. Status of these anomalies and their detection are monitored through

Process Control Charts and Metric Application Techniques. These PQI's are each potential 1st Pass Yield points and can be used as either internal or external customer scorecard venues. In doing this, it changes the emphasis on hardware non-conformances from:

Detection → Prevention
(Inspector)   (Quality Engineer)

In Method:

The application of PQI's implement Statistical Techniques which identify, monitor and control the failure / defects at each PQI point identified within the total manufacturing functional flow. If used as a 1st Pass Yield Indicator, the PQI becomes a dual trend setter as operation status indicators and work center Cost of Poor Quality indicator.

In Practice:

A diagram of the entire manufacturing functional flow is laid out and PQI's are identified within each operational process for monitoring and reporting (see Figure 5-1). QA takes ownership of all non-conformances and establishes a Preliminary Material Review. The non-conforming material enters a locked-up bonded status or MRB (Material Review Board) and is held for disposition to root cause and corrective action. Immediate "as Built" resolution of current operation non-conformances moves the emphasis to a Preventative awareness thus improving the yield and lowering the 1st Pass Inspection findings away from the Detection posture. This is accomplished with higher success with the Quality Engineering (QE) organization teaming with the respective functional organizations to disposition the non-conformances to a Corrective and Preventative manner. The QE would then have the responsibility to follow up with the Verification of Non-recurrence and verify the fix was completed. This would be an absolute Closed Loop System.

A standard method for logging and disposition of a finding at a PQI is implemented through a Defect and Corrective Action

Data Collection System and metric reporting through Data Acquisition and Trend Analysis.

Proper and constructive metrics reporting is the biggest hurtle.

Once data starts being collected, then every possible type of report and chart is thought of, requested and developed.

Out of this effort a new department is born called Quality Data Systems or Quality Systems.

This new department can typically consist of a manager, one or two data analysts, possibly a data entry clerk and maybe a quality engineer and become a real overkill.

Remember the K.I.S.S. Rule (Keep It Simple Stupid)

Present the information (Data) in a total Visual Continuity (Eye to Brain coordination) like Stop Light Charts or Functional Flow Charts with linear color flows.

The use of a Performance Metrics format, like the OPM (Oregon Productivity Matrix) that the University of Oregon developed or KPM (Key Performance Metrics), Pareto's which identify specific category types or commodities and defect / reject charts.

These are successful means of communicating a broad picture in easy-to-understand display.

Do not post raw data or page reports or filled out Quality forms as display board metrics.

No one has or takes the time to read data and the time it takes to update and maintain it is Non-Value-Added Work.

The common mistake most Business Leadership Management Teams embrace is, when it comes to data, "*More is better*".

Metrics should always be reported in simple and user understandable content and format as possible.

In most every situation, the format and content are expressed in high technical terms and statistical format; like reading a corporate financial statement or the graphs from the stock exchange report.

Not only boring, but uninformative and interpretative to everyone outside the creator's venue.

Even though the collecting and maintaining of Data and its transfer to charts and reports does require a somewhat analytical and computer literate skill set, it by no means requires what most businesses put in place with a degreed Statistician or Quality Engineer to perform the function.

A well-trained Data or Administrative Clerk could do the job quite sufficiently and give them a purpose of fulfilment beyond pushing paper and getting coffee for the boss and his staff.

The author has managed many Quality Data System functions within QA Organizations and in a wide variety of business settings; in only a few companies, was it required to have the Data System functions performed by degreed individuals.

These few companies had large corporate infrastructure and organizations, very wasteful in their process structures, job descriptions and requirement for highly technical personnel doing lower-level analytical job tasks.

Somehow, in the minds of the corporate thinkers, they equate Data Analysis, Trend Reporting and Manipulation of such things to a GENIUS personality type and really believe it's a proven scientific means to Quality Improvement.

Every time budget cuts or reduction in work force have to occur, and management is looking for Non-Value-Added resources to eliminate, they always hone in on such things as Document Control, Inspection, clerical and the need for all the Data Systems statistics (Trending charts and SPC) and concluded it is not actually contributing one dime's worth of investment towards the profit share of the business.

What usually ends up happening after the layoffs and elimination of the resource and support for these functions, is routing the data gathering and reporting to each individual Functional Organization's responsibility, handed over to some department clerk or just stopped all together.

Quality Assurance under their charter maintains reporting of non-conformances and corrective actions, defects and reject findings, while each functional group reports on their activities separately; and I might add to a minimum.

All of the bloated organizational activities are reduced to what it should have been in the first place and the Data Systems activities are managed and reported by each functional organization.

The best way to coordinate and report on it as a whole, is in a monthly PMR's (Program Management Review) or Business Reviews with the Leadership Team.

It is noteworthy to mention that some form of data collection at PQI Points is required to subsequently control output of First Pass Yield, non-conformances and for management to have visibility into the inner workings of the business and the problem areas.

Metrics best serve the company if instead of creating a separate organizational infrastructure such as Data Services, that each department has ownership of their own and a general assembly of the leadership team meets to discuss and assign actions accordingly.

The key to successfully using PQI's, is working IMMEDIATELY on the anomaly findings, and enter into a Trend Analysis Database where the data can be used to report and analyze the PQI data.

The First Pass Yield data should be viewed as a metric indicator. Be sure to Post your Metrics out on the Production Floor Area where the FPY Indicator is.

If you have <98% First Pass Yield (at the 3 Sigma Level), then this is a good indicator that there are problems within the entire Operation Build sequence, and a high Rework and Scrap Cost indicative.

This could also point to "Hidden Factory" presumptions.

Nevertheless, Cost of Poor Quality would be high and positive RCCA (Root Cause Corrective Action) should be implemented through a CAB (Corrective Action Board), which is chaired by QA who performs the Closed-Loop function of Verification for Non-recurrence through the Quality Engineering organization.

A follow-up activity to recourse improvement out of the CAB would be Preventative Actions with those issues identified as systemic or repeat trend offenders.

The proper forum for this would be a PAB (Preventative Action Board) which is chaired by Engineering and QA is a member of.

The key consideration should be to improve the First Pass Yield throughput and lower non-conformance findings.

How to raise First Pass Yield:

- **Identifying** the Hidden Factory (Rework, Scrap and Warranty)→

- **Implement** a tool to gather data on Process Quality Indicators and report respective Trend Analysis for Corrective Actions →

- **Incorporate** Preventative Action Plans and Lesson's Learned→

- **Eliminate** the Hidden Factory →

- **Improve** Process Productivity (PQI)→ · **Increase** First Pass Yield throughput

As a Functional Process improves, the PQI Nodes can decrease.

This gives a positive indication within specific operations of a functional process flow, if there are improvements by the operators, assemblers, workers, in doing self-inspection and taking ownership of the product, they have responsibility to manufacture and build to print.

This would indicate higher skill set and accountability of their training to perform the tasks and job functions under their assignment.

It helps eliminate the need for QC Inspection functions within the functional process flow and the reduction of the PQIs in that flow, as QC is being presented with better and better product, or a service is improving at satisfying their customer with a higher performance rate.

Once again, it's all about **Application** and <u>not **Substance**</u>.

This is where the best scenario for a productive and "Value Added" QA Organization is found, with a majority-based Quality Engineering activity.

The QC Receiving Inspection and Final Inspection activities should not be the mainstay of the QA Functional Support or Service to any business.

The Work-In-Process (WIP) should only dictate one or two Inspectors to support the functional compliance verification.

The QE's support the Material Review Board activity and Preliminary Disposition as delegated by the MRB Chairperson, as well as overseeing the WIP activity for technical and non-conformance issues.

QE also assists Manufacturing Engineers in identifying production resolutions under build to print and specification compliance and being a resource to interface with Engineering on design to manufacturing improvements.

QE has the horsepower to imposing the Quality Agenda and is the juggernaut of the organization, but the real advantage of having an expert non-engineering technical resource, is to interface with the customers and government ACO on compliance and acceptance issues.

How the QA Organization as a department is structured and the functional assignment of each person is identified and assigned by Primary and Secondary responsibilities must be clearly laid out and defined.

The most typical QA Organizations in any manufacturing business are based around QC Inspection activities.

This is just the opposite of what an efficiently organized, "Quality" mindset, company would do.

You want to move away from QC Inspection being prominent and depended upon for checking each and every part, so production and assembly can rework to print instead of building to print.

The order must be to move away from **Detection** (needing QC verification of Build to Print) towards → **Prevention** (Production verifying built to print then submitting to Inspection for sample buy-off) Zero Defects-100% First Pass Yield.

Nevertheless, with most companies, depending on their size and volume of sales, the amount of QC Inspection support varies.

Most small to mid-size (50-500 employee) companies QA Organizational Charts have a QA Manager, with a Receiving, In-Process and Final Inspection, Calibration Lab, a supervisor over those Inspectors and a Quality Engineer or two.

Larger to corporate size (1000+ employee) companies QA Organizational Charts have a Director of Quality, and in larger corporate size company's a Vice President of Quality, with a QA Manager, Quality Engineers (Hardware & Software), Receiving, In-Process and Final Inspection, QC Supervisor, Calibration Lab, Quality Data Systems, Internal Auditing, Supplier Quality (Supply Chain) and Testing.

Sometimes you'll combine other activities which require close monitoring or controlled environment which need to be placed under the QA department's Independent Flag and ACO Authority, like Document Control or Configuration Management.

The proper usage of any QA Organization is to lead and mentor the Quality protocols throughout the business organizational infrastructure and to enhance Quality as a synonymous function within every organization throughout the business.

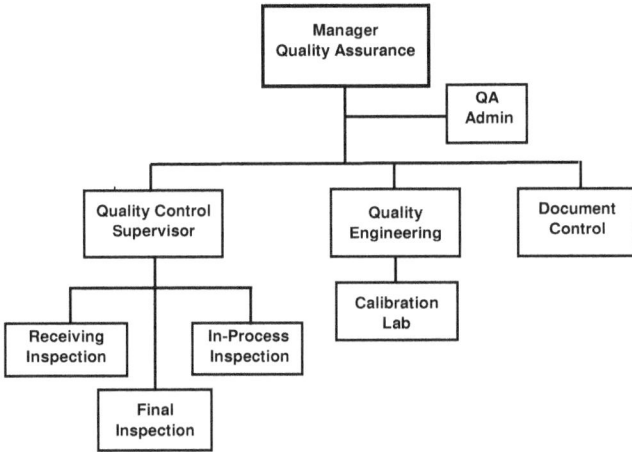

Figure 5-2 Typical Small – Mid Size Company QA
Organization

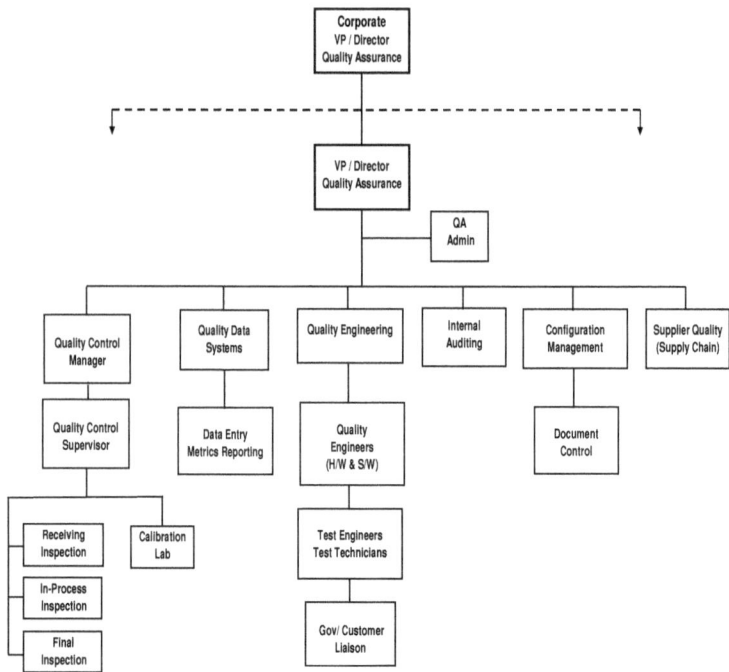

Figure 5-3 Typical Large Company QA Organization and Infrastructure

To maintain Quality as a separate department or function greatly limits a company's ability to impose any Quality Improvement Program or move a Quality agenda into each department in a unison self-sufficient manner, bringing the message and mindset that:

"Quality is Everything!"

WALSTON RULE #6

"Your job is to make me successful,
my job is to help you get me there"

What would you imagine happens when a person gives up on themselves?

I truly hope that no one reading this can actually answer that question.

There's a lot of pain and suffering in it.

I've had the distinct opportunity in counseling individuals and mentoring those who have lost all Hope and were at a place in their lives of completely giving up and even contemplating ending their lives; but that's another topic for another book.

Nevertheless, the main theme behind each experience was an emotional detachment of the individual's ability to contribute in achieving their hearts desires or being productive and satisfied in the environment surrounding them.

Losing Hope is a pitiful thing.

Hope is one of the three Virtues of God and imparted through the human spirit as a characteristic that all humans are born with; it resides in the unseen reaches of our minds and dreams.

To lose Hope is to lose an intrinsic part of your soul.

Exploring the possibilities of Hope is endless.

How extensively and deep can you dream or conjure up ideas is where it begins.

It's that inner spark of hyperactive sensitivity which gives you energy and strengthens you to overcome doubt.

Hope destroys Fear.

It is the opposite of oppression and says "Yes" to Faith and embraces Love.

The taker of Hope is Doubt, or the sarcastic reality of Doubt, which comes out of the mouths of so many close to us, in such graphic flavors as:

What about: *"if you keep going the way you're going, then you're going straight to hell!"*
A statement that there is still some Hope of changing, if...

What about: *"Mr. Smith, we're sorry, but the final test results came back and there's no doubt, we estimate you have three months to live; we suggest you get your affairs in order."*
A statement where fact becomes fear and tries to kill all chance of Hope.

What about: *"I don't want to burst your bubble, but don't you think you're a little bit out of your league with that idea; I mean you're no Donald Trump."*
A statement which fosters doubt through a sarcastic innuendo. Could be said out of jealousy.

What about: *"You'll never become anything, you're just like your father/mother.   He/she never became anything either, always had his/her head in the clouds."*
A statement which is used much too often towards children to entice them to do better but may cause despair and a feeling of Hopelessness in individuals with low self-esteem.

These kinds of sabotaging comments are used in business settings as well, when dealing with employees, colleagues and even from customers.

It's extremely important to realize that Hope fosters a productive Quality environment and seeds the growth of prosperity.

It starts at the individual level and passes over into group and team settings.

Hope is the cornerstone of any Quality Improvement activity or idea that stretches one's imagination to do something outside the norm.

The desire behind innovative thinking relies on the individual energy of a person's Hopeful belief, that the idea they are putting forth will be successful.

Part of the responsibility of management or any leadership role and function is to foster a Hopeful environment for their fellow employees or constituents.

Access to functional resources, funding, education and training, facilities, recreation and a good communication forum, is essential to building and maintaining any Quality Improvement Process.

Key Indicators of a failed business environment are:

1-Increased Non-Conformances and MRB Activity, **2**-Bad Attitudes, **3**-Overworked Employees, **4**-Stressed Reactions to questions, **5**-Only a Few Main Contributors who constantly are asked to do the majority of task assignments, **6**-Increased Open Management Positions (especially in the QA Department), **7**- Having a Union in-Place with (80% plus) of the work force associated with it, and lastly, **8**-Unfavorable Judgments against outstanding Litigations.

So, an indication of a healthy business environment would be the opposite of these, with the added focus by management to enforce Quality Centric Policies and Procedures throughout the business.

Since the 1990's, International Consortiums' have been able to change the face of Quality requirements and standards world-wide.

A huge impact in the United States occurred within businesses that dealt with Aerospace and Department of Defense contracts with the introduction of ISO and suspension of the Mil-Standards.

With it came a significant attempt to change the roles and responsibilities of the "Quality Manager", which is the common lead role within the Quality Assurance organization and in most businesses, the leadership position as the Quality Management Representative (QMR).

The focus attempt which would be known in the industry as "Forward Thinkers", was nothing more than the attempt to institutionalize QA from a Support Service Organization, with the authority as the Internal Customer, into a Scholastic Trainer of Process, Procedures and Audits.

The idea I believe started out well founded, but because of career path bureaucrats from the Institutions of Higher Minutia, who infiltrated the production manufacturing industries, pushed their political influences into accepted policies by the executive management of major corporations. This is where focus groups and steering committees began springing forth Quality agendas, which flowed down new standards of business practices.

The focus of what the "Quality Manager" roles and functions internally are, for at least the first part of the 21st Century, is definitely quite different than those of the fifty years previous to that.

A new role being expounded on the "Quality Manager" of the 21st Century is that of a Business Manager.

Most, if not the majority of corporate style businesses, have an Executive Management Team which in the past was all about the Business Sales and Marketing, Finance, President/CEO, Engineering, Ops Management running the company and setting the Policies and Business Plan Agenda.

Now, as the management infrastructure changes to include a Business Management setting, each organization within the business must be represented in the Executive Staff, which includes Quality Assurance (QA).

QA now gets involved with the company visions (Policy and Mission Statement), business agendas and financials, company-wide improvement programs and training.

There was a gentleman by the name of Peter Drucker, who was labeled at one time as "The man who invented management".

A documented and published writer, management consultant, and self-described "social ecologist of the Mid to Late 20th Century.

I knew of him from my old Alma Mater, the University of New York (NYU) where he was a Professor of Management Studies.

His work and writings were famous and legendary within business and scholastic circles.

In 1963, Mr. Drucker published an article in the Harvard Business Review entitled, "Managing for Business Effectiveness".

The emphasis that Drucker made in this article was that the first duty of a Business Manager is "to strive for the best possible economic results from the resources currently employed."

He expounded later on this by stating that the Business Manager's job is "to direct resources towards opportunities for economically significant results."

In my career as a Quality Management professional, I must agree that as a part of the Business Management Team, the Quality Manager must also view his responsibility to the economic control and welfare of the business.

Notwithstanding, his primary role within the QA Charter is to serve as the liaison between the Customer/Regulatory compliance requirements and guarantee 100% compliance to acceptability of the end product delivery to the Contract SOW / Purchase Order requirements.

If under Drucker's consideration, every manager in the business is a "Business Manager" and that title enables the primary interest of each manager to be one of economic stewardship, above their descriptive roles and discipline, then Quality would be inherently compromised.

You can not serve two Masters of Emphasis, "Quality is Everything" and "Profit is Everything".

The two can and must work together to achieve one goal...building and maintaining a Product Quality reputation, while gaining a fair and reasonable profit without compromising the value of Quality in every product sold.

This would be the strategy of a sound business policy, with assurance towards Quality and Customer Satisfaction, which in my opinion, is what gives a business safeguards towards economic growth.

With the advent of the 21st Century, the Aerospace Quality Manager has moved into or embedded within the Program Management function as a part of that organizational support team.

The idea was to get all of the Functional Organizations into a huddle mode and controlled by the Program Office so product flow and release to final delivery could be scheduled and controlled by the Roll-Through determination of one source, the Program Management Office (PMO).

The problem with that concept is that the QA Organization (Department) is not a Functional Organization; they are a Support Service and Compliance Chartered Organization, whose directive is to, without constraint by any outside organization, be independent of business decisions which could inherently cause product to be non-conforming to the customers compliance requirements.

QA is supposed to be that Safe-Guard between Program Office and Production Operations work arounds of Regulatory and Compliance Requirements just to ship product to On-Time Delivery (OTD) schedules.

The traditional roles of QA as being a bunch of Inspectors (COPS) writing tickets and issuing non-conformance tags, moved into the program centric role of supporting specific contract requirements and meeting the On-Dock delivery dates according to Production and Contract Waterfall schedules.

This helped place the burden of supporting the Customer agenda of deliveries onto the QA Organization Management by making them part of the Program Management Team and under the guise of the Program Office Directorate.

Nevertheless, the QA organizational charter and authority to act independently as the "Eyes and the Ears" of the Customer when related to non-conformances and compliance with Design to Build requirements, still stands and must be considered as disassociated with Program Office as well as Upper Management Directive.

No matter how interactive QA is with the Program Office or any other functional organization, they have autonomy as an extension of the Customers Compliance and Regulatory Representative.

The hands-on aspects of QA and the Value-Added resource of Quality Engineering to be a Technical Arm of the Design and Manufacture Engineering functions, transitioned (or more accurately morphed) into Auditors, Six Sigma metric desk jockeys and Steering Committee Participants.

Over emphasis of QA transitioning into these kinds of functions actually depletes their role as the Internal Customer by changing the mindset of QA's function from Compliance to Conformance.

The healthy mix for QA is to have Quality Engineers embedded on the Production Assembly Floor, teaming with the Manufacturing Engineers, investigating and fixing the Non-Conformance issues, leading Continuous Improvement Action Committees, training and mentoring Inspection Personnel, Heading Sigma Projects and over-seeing the processes and participating in LEAN initiatives to eliminate the Non-conformance Root Causes and thus moving the paradigm towards **Prevention** Awareness.

The less Detection (Inspection) Processes that are implemented throughout the Production Cycle, the more Compliance related the Production Assembly Processes becomes.

In the Production mindset, Inspection (Detection) always means someone else checks my work and identifies the Findings (Non-Conformances).

In the Quality mindset, Production Self-Inspection (Prevention) always means you check your own work and submit to Inspection (Internal Customer) with the mindset of 100% Compliance and 100% First Pass Yield.

In many companies, Manufacturing Production/Assembly have their own internal Checkers (Inspectors) that do "First Build" Inspections and do the interface of defect findings and any rework training with the operator that built the product. This ensures a higher level of acceptability when the product is finally passed on to a QC Inspection Point and ensures a higher FPY for that Cell Manufacturing Flow.

QA should always impose a Zero Tolerance policy for Detection and Defects.

Push the responsibility back on the functional organizations who build the product to build it right and QA to do an Average Quality Level (AQL) inspect of the Key and Critical characteristics as outlined by the Design Engineering criteria (Drawing, Product Spec's, etc).

The Prevention Awareness attitude brings into perspective, something that has been a catchphrase for Quality Assurance and "Quality" as a euphemism, "Doing the Right Thing".

It implies that everyone must be held to task for "Doing the Right Thing" and QA must catch what is not being done right and make it so.

There's that Watch-Dog over-seer function which is inherently assigned to QA and assumed to be the outcome of what "Quality" promotes as a discipline and instills as a function.

So, how many other disciplines like "QA" are there out there, in the industrial business arena, which coincide with Quality's mission objective.

The answer is a shocking "Zero".

As a functional attribute and measurement of excellence or as an organizational function to ensure compliance towards achieving excellence, "QA" stands alone.

The "Stable" condition aspired under any normal and healthy human circumstance, is a positive acceptable measurement.

One that promotes an outcome we call "Good".

We even go so far as to promote extenuating levels of "Good" labeled as: "Very Good", "Excellent" or "Outstanding", and then there's the ultimate expression of "Superior".

The normality for the level of measurement of "Good", is the Mean Average of the full expression of its applied attribute, as being applied to any situation or circumstance.

This sets the baseline for Upper and Lower limits of "Good" (Acceptability).

This is accomplished by doing what Dr. Deming called "Doing the Right Thing" and producing acceptable product and services, which the customer and consumer can classify as "Good" and the extenuating levels associated with it.

Unacceptable or Non-Conforming product and services is considered as "BAD".

"Bad" measures below the lowest acceptable limit of the "Good" baseline.

Even so, there are also extenuating levels of "BAD", which are categorized as: "Very Bad", Extremely Bad", "Unsatisfactory", with the ultimate expression of "Totally Crap" or Scrap.

Under any circumstances or conditions, where the Claim to Fame is given to excellence in performance, skill set or ability, the expected outcome is always measured by the level of "Quality" achieved, but it will be to "Quality" and nothing else.

The great American mindset is, "if you're not first, then your last"; there is no second place for being a "Winner".

If you'll accept second best, then you will compromise "Quality" with everything you do.

It should be clear that unacceptable anything is "Not Good" and the aspiration to successful business or Life Practices is achieving through "Doing the Right Thing" and producing "Good" result; and the reason for that is because,

"Quality is Everything!"

WALSTON RULE #7
"Get away from trying to solve the problems,
start working the issues"

Team Concept

The Team concept has been with us since the beginning of human interaction.

When the talents of two or more people joined together to find a solution to an issue or a single idea was developed into a practical application, then the Team Concept came into play.

Where more than one person was needed to apply the application of a process to produce a product or join in exchange of ideas to formulate a concept and implement the idea into reality, then the Team Concept was introduced.

If you want a definition of what a Team is, then I've concluded that it is – *a Group of individuals linked in a common goal and or purpose.*

Now a Group does not necessarily constitute a Team.

It should consist of members with complementary skills.

In many instances, a group of people coming together without a common purpose and without complementary skills turns into a Mob.

In a business setting, it is the primary objective of the Executive Management Team to establish the policies, business plan and mission objective(s) which run the business infrastructure and flow these as objectives downward through the middle management and supervisory hierarchy throughout the functional organizations.

The Team's secondary supporters which promote the functions of the primary goals are known as Stakeholders.

Stakeholders are individuals who directly affect an organization or assist in assignments within a Team's function.

In the minds of most people, there are usually two scenarios automatically thought of or identified with when speaking about what a Team is: The Military or Sports.

Both consist of well-trained, strictly organized individuals with a common goal or purpose.

As you watch these teams execute their mission, you can't help having a feeling that they will be successful.

Part of that is because they are so well trained and their skill set so well defined, that they are considered Experts in what they do.

To be brought into their Team would require an elite individual, who could meet the same qualifications of their high standards and discipline.

Another part of the Team concept is Loyalty.

Loyalty invites a willingness to sacrifice.

Take the Family Unit as a perfect example of a Team collective order and loyalty.

The Family goes beyond individuals working or living together.

These people share a common blood tie with each other; who have the same DNA.

Again, it is supposed that people with a common goal or purpose will support each other in achieving such things.

The loyalty factor plays a big part in securing the steadfastness of the Team's success.

The final aspect to consider with any Team formation is Leadership.

When dealing with Human Group Interaction, it can be like herding cats if a focus and direction is not maintained.

A group leader should be assigned to manage the Team agenda and keep the focus on a projected goal and outcome.

A perfect example of this would be the election of a Jury Foreman for a Trial Jury.

A Trial Jury can become very debating and splinter off in many directions with opinions and facts but never reach a unanimous conclusion for a verdict.

The Foreman's job is to manage the Team in keeping the focus towards the goal of a unanimous decision without dictating the outcome of the decision; the Foreman has a single vote as well within the Team, but not the final say.

Teams are not always formed for the right reasons.

The mandate of the Team must be concisely delegated and effortlessly coordinated.

The structured organization and workings of a Team can have misconceptions associated with it.

The kind of Team which is a membership between colleagues, or a business Leadership Management is what I refer to as a *Fraternal Social Alliance*.

These are policy setters and tend to see the business or membership colleague from a thirty-thousand-foot perspective and their involvement is very high-level management attributed.

A Team should never be formed to forego the individual dictation or decision of an Expert within a functional discipline.

Too many times, within a business setting, Teams are formed to solve problems which are specific to a single functional organizations' responsibility.

If by management edict, the Team formation has been given the charter and authority to insight change, and in doing so the outcome affects the authority and functionality of a respective organization, then the outcome is most likely undermining that organization's infrastructure and authority.

Unless the organization in which the changes are being imposed has the lead in the decision-making process, then it may be out of step with their contract, business requirements and/or industry protocols which may violate its purpose and existence within the business structure.

As an example: for Program Management to form a Team with participants from all the functional organizations to look into why the Material Review Board (MRB) has so many parts in QA Bond and discuss why QA is viewed as the bottleneck because of this, then that would be the wrong reason for a Team formation.

On the other hand, if the Program Management wanted to form a Team to look into Improvements on functional organizations (Internal Sources) or Suppliers (External Sources) that were producing high reject rate parts (which were being identified through the MRB and causing increased levels of Scrap and Rework) then this would have a profound insight into the Root Causes and lead to individual Focus Group Actions to resolve real issues and problems for Corrective and Preventative Action.

Again, consensus by a Team group decision is not always positive and is usually intrusive within functional organization infrastructures.

The Team Concept of improvement is best utilized within a Project Concept Model.

The Team Concept of Management Leadership Interaction is best utilized with assignments of Projects and Problem Solving within the ranks of their Functional Organization Management.

Never form a Team or develop a Team Strategy towards a Functional Organizations authority or business responsibility, always use the Team Concept towards Project Level activities to resolve Issues and Problems.

Working an Issue

An Issue is a condition that has lesser impact and core value than a Problem but is still a non-conformance and has circumstances which gives it venue to a quick fix and quick resolve in order to keep the condition from becoming a Problem.

Many times, an Issue can be an observation or suggestion and placed on a Parking Lot Chart and worked when time and resources are available, but in most situations, it is best to resolve an Issue as soon as possible.

Three (3) elements of working an Issue:

1) Identify a Single Issue to be worked, not multiples (stick to a single issue only)
2) Involve Experts and identify all the Stakeholders
3) Get to a Quick solution and Fix ASAP!

Approach any subsets which branch off the original issue as New Issues and follow the three-element flow for those as well.

Don't get caught up in long laborious meetings or conversations brainstorming an issue.

Research and get the facts through hands-on investigation.

In my opinion and experience, nothing destroys a Team's centric strength, motion, and ability to fulfill its purpose more than individuals within it not engaging in hands-on, one-on-one activities. Desk-Jockey's don't work.

There are always a few whose butts are stuck to their office chairs, hunched over a laptop all day, preparing useless charts and reports, or preparing for one unproductive meeting after another.

But thank God, you will have within your organization, those few individuals who roll up their sleeves, hit the floor and do the hard work of actually interfacing with the stakeholders, changing and improving the processes and managing the corrective action activities to a final resolution, with verification of non-recurrence, making sure the root cause corrective action got implemented and fixed the condition.

All in all, the old saying, "that's one less issue I have to deal with", is a true and sustaining mindset.

Solving Problems

Problems are the extreme condition of any situation and are best resolved using a Root Cause Corrective Action (RCCA) venue approach.

The most accepted approach to any Problem Solving is through logical analysis of the finding or deviation identified.

All Problems must have a conclusion based on the findings with evidence (facts and data), method to grasp the situation, contain the observations and data, build on conclusions, report the findings and confirm the Problem Resolution and Effectivity.

The problem with Problem Solving is the Why's can go on in seemingly, endless branching directions.

A process that the author would promote as efficient and effective would be the,

Five Principles of Problem-Solving Method.

1) The Finding (Detailed Problem Definition) - Who, What, When, Where and Why.

2) Root Cause (5 Why's Analysis) Investigation – Ishikawa Fishbone Point of Cause (Figure 7-1)

3) Immediate Corrective Action (Containment)

4) Long-Term Corrective Action (Elimination of the Findings Root Cause)

5) Verification of Non-Recurrence (Problem completely fixed and verified)

PROBLEM: To Many Failures on Assembly Line

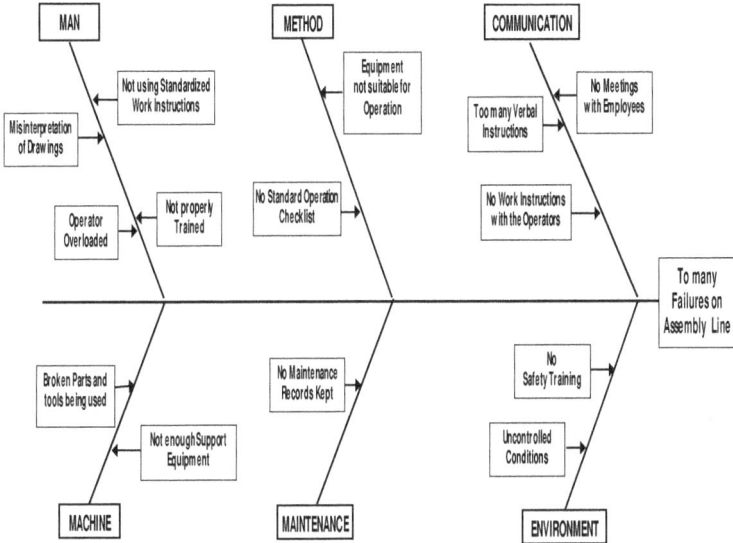

MAN

METHOD

COMMUNICATION

Not using Standardized Work Instructions

Equipment not suitable for Operation

No Meetings with Employees

Misinterpretation of Drawings

Too many Verbal Instructions

Operator Overloaded

Not properly Trained

No Standard Operation Checklist

No Work Instructions with the Operators

To many Failures on Assembly Line

Broken Parts and tools being used

No Maintenance Records Kept

No Safety Training

Not enough Support Equipment

Uncontrolled Conditions

MACHINE

MAINTENANCE

ENVIRONMENT

Figure 7-1   Ishikawa Fishbone - Root Cause Analysis Diagram

In conjunction with the Fishbone Diagram and layout of the six (6) respective category conditions associated with the Root Cause, there is the 5 WHY Drilldown categories and the splinter conditions identified for each.

From this there could be countless other adages, like breakaway Six Sigma Projects or LEAN initiatives, all of which can be massively time consuming, costly and an overkill to solving the problem, especially in a minor situation.

Definition should be given to items 2, 3, and 4 under the Five Principles, so there is no confusion.

These three elements of the Problem-Solving formula are the aspects behind RCCA and must be given full resource to answering the Point of Cause Drilldown.

Root Cause – The underlying or original cause of an incident, issue, problem or non-conformance, which if adequately addressed, will prevent the non-conformance from re-occurring.

Immediate Corrective Action – Immediate containment actions that will isolate the problem and protect the customer or next operation from non-conformances until long term Corrective Action is implemented.

Long-Term Corrective Action – Actions taken to ensure the Root Cause is eliminated and prevented from re-occurring.

This method was intended to be a drilled down scientific approach to every pathway end possible, which could relate itself to the original Problem scenario.

Build a complete picture of the Problem Pathway and hopefully come to the Root Cause.

The first and foremost effort and resource must be given to the investigation and analysis of the Root Cause and the Drilldown explanations which will help lead to the Corrective Action task assignments.

The only caution in using these models, is that once these kinds of process models are implemented into the business as accepted practices for problem solving and corrective actions, then every non-conformance situation becomes a problem and is approached using these initiatives.

The caution comes from using large scale RCCA with small scale issues.

Each situation must be classified by priority in order to utilize resources accordingly.

"Issues" should not express the level of RCCA that a "Problem" commands.

What can happen is another extension to the QA Organization or a new department is born and staffed to support this effort.

Usually called Statistical Process Control (SPC), Corrective Action Board (CAB), Cost of Poor Quality or Preventative Action Committee, it can be only the tip of the iceberg when it comes to creating and supporting the infrastructure for collecting, monitoring and reporting data on Non-conformances.

Figure 7-2 gives a sample of what a 5 WHY Drilldown would look like, taken from the category examples in Figure 7-1.

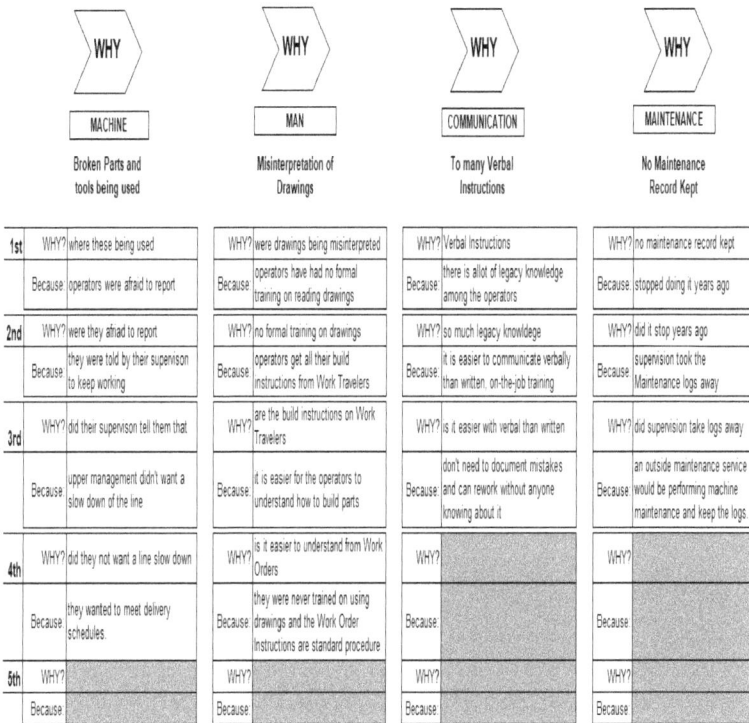

	MACHINE	MAN	COMMUNICATION	MAINTENANCE
WHY	WHY	WHY	WHY	WHY
	Broken Parts and tools being used	Misinterpretation of Drawings	To many Verbal Instructions	No Maintenance Record Kept
1st WHY?	where these being used	were drawings being misinterpreted	Verbal Instructions	no maintenance record kept
Because:	operators were afraid to report	operators have had no formal training on reading drawings	there is allot of legacy knowledge among the operators	stopped doing it years ago
2nd WHY?	were they afraid to report	no formal training on drawings	so much legacy knowledge	did it stop years ago
Because:	they were told by their supervision to keep working	operators get all their build instructions from Work Travelers	it is easier to communicate verbally than written, on-the-job training	supervision took the Maintenance logs away
3rd WHY?	did their supervision tell them that	are the build instructions on Work Travelers	is it easier with verbal than written	did supervision take logs away
Because:	upper management didn't want a slow down of the line	it is easier for the operators to understand how to build parts	don't need to document mistakes and can rework without anyone knowing about it	an outside maintenance service would be performing machine maintenance and keep the logs.
4th WHY?	did they not want a line slow down	is it easier to understand from Work Orders	WHY?	WHY?
Because:	they wanted to meet delivery schedules.	they were never trained on using drawings and the Work Order instructions are standard procedure	Because:	Because:
5th WHY?	WHY?	WHY?	WHY?	WHY?
Because:	Because:	Because:	Because:	Because:

Figure 7-2   5-WHYs Point of Cause Drilldown

The bottom-line with any Problem is to get to the Root Cause and fix it immediately before you build more bad product and waste more money.

Quality and Cost go hand-in-hand with non-conformances and the elimination of such.

Work

Let's look at work as a process and how to improve the Structure and Process of Work.

There have been tons of studies done on Work and the mechanics behind what Work is.

In any structured work setting, within any environment, the common theme to categorize the elements behind what Work is, comes down to three aspects:

1) **Necessary Work**,
2) **Unnecessary Work**,
3) **Not Working**

Necessary Work is partitioned into Value Added and Non-Value Added.

Unnecessary Work is partitioned into Rework and All Others.

Not Working is a stand-alone category.
Standard definitions follow beneath each category
(see Figure 7-3).

If you wanted to define what the intent of Work is, I've concluded that it is *"the amount of effort applied to accomplish any anatomic function or task which uses energy and resource to do so."*

In physics, Work is applied in mechanical terms as "the amount of energy transferred by a force acting through a distance" and like energy, it is a scalar quantity.

The equation would be,

$$W = F \cdot d = Fd \cos\theta$$

that Force (F) displaced by distance (d) acts in parallel to each other and the angle between the force and the displacement vector (θ) must remain constant and linear in direction.

Nevertheless, the outcome of work whether it be anatomic or mechanical, is the same and is based on anticipated results.

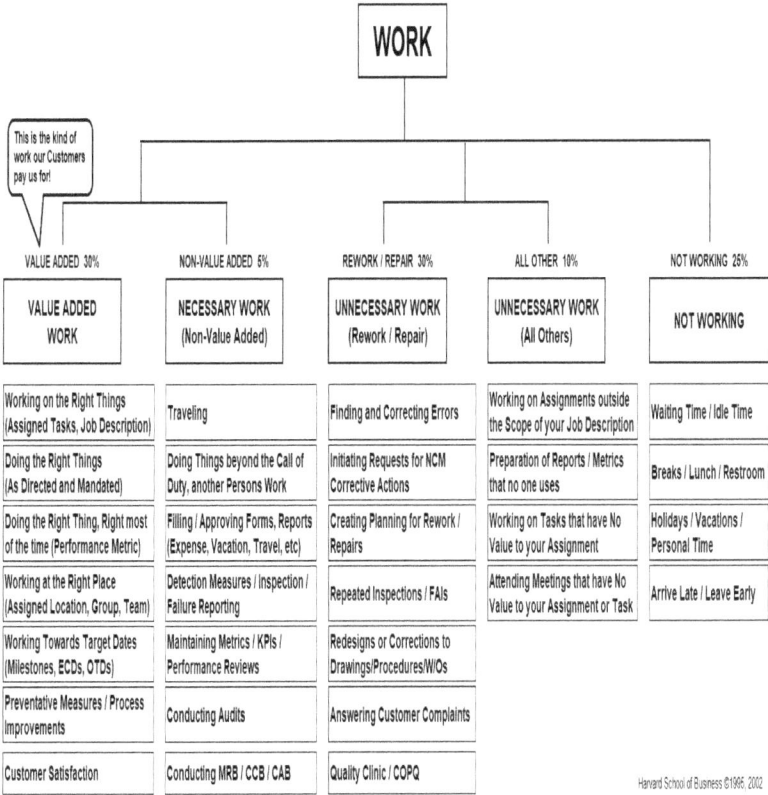

WORK

This is the kind of work our Customers pay us for!

VALUE ADDED 30%	NON-VALUE ADDED 5%	REWORK / REPAIR 30%	ALL OTHER 10%	NOT WORKING 25%
VALUE ADDED WORK	**NECESSARY WORK** (Non-Value Added)	**UNNECESSARY WORK** (Rework / Repair)	**UNNECESSARY WORK** (All Others)	**NOT WORKING**
Working on the Right Things (Assigned Tasks, Job Description)	Traveling	Finding and Correcting Errors	Working on Assignments outside the Scope of your Job Description	Waiting Time / Idle Time
Doing the Right Things (As Directed and Mandated)	Doing Things beyond the Call of Duty, another Persons Work	Initiating Requests for NCM Corrective Actions	Preparation of Reports / Metrics that no one uses	Breaks / Lunch / Restroom
Doing the Right Thing, Right most of the time (Performance Metric)	Filling / Approving Forms, Reports (Expense, Vacation, Travel, etc)	Creating Planning for Rework / Repairs	Working on Tasks that have No Value to your Assignment	Holidays / Vacations / Personal Time
Working at the Right Place (Assigned Location, Group, Team)	Detection Measures / Inspection / Failure Reporting	Repeated Inspections / FAIs	Attending Meetings that have No Value to your Assignment or Task	Arrive Late / Leave Early
Working Towards Target Dates (Milestones, ECDs, OTDs)	Maintaining Metrics / KPIs / Performance Reviews	Redesigns or Corrections to Drawings/Procedures/W/Os		
Preventative Measures / Process Improvements	Conducting Audits	Answering Customer Complaints		
Customer Satisfaction	Conducting MRB / CCB / CAB	Quality Clinic / COPQ		

Harvard School of Business ©1996, 2002

Figure 7-3 Work Category Breakdown

Work as a process should always be based around highest Quality expectations and applied with the highest level of training and available resources to do each and every task to fullest succession.

When Work is expended on a wasteful cause, such as Rework and Repair, correcting errors and mistakes, follow-up audits, RCCA's, follow-up meetings and useless metrics reporting, then you are flushing your profits down the toilet and overstressing and overworking your business resources.

It is a repeated scenario, time and time again and we see it every time we drive past a business and see a "For Lease" sign in the window.

The Customer

It's the one thing you want more than life itself when you start a business and the worst nightmare for any business when things go south.

The Customer is subjective, at best, as far as true importance when you're in business.

In my not so humble opinion, the Customer is not always right and not always desired.

It depends on the Customer, just like it depends on the Supplier when you are the Customer.

Way too many business owners and executive management employees put priority emphasis on the Customer's opinion or desires above their own business capabilities or profit.

I can't tell you how many times over my career that I've worked for companies, who have killed their employees just to satisfy a Bad Customers desire or ego, just to keep their business and lose money doing so.

Sometimes the smart thing to do is cut your losses, dump the Bad Customer and reorganize your catalog and business plan to something that you can do with less resource, non-conformances and profit share.

Live within your means and stop looking to grow so big that all you're doing is planning yourself out of business; smaller can be better if it means you keep your business.

I was given something awhile back that was supposed to enlighten me on the importance of the "Customer"; it's a perspective which is a little too heavy on the appeasement side and I have some disagreements.

The credit for this enlightenment is supposedly from Gandhi himself, but I'm not sure of that.

Nevertheless, here's what was pronounced:

"A customer is the most important visitor on our premises. He is not dependent on us. We are dependent on him. He is not an interruption of our work. He is the purpose of it. He is not an outsider to our business. He is part of it. We are not doing him a favour by serving him. He is doing us a favour by giving us the opportunity to do so."

In keeping with true form as a conservative, I've made my own statement of enlightenment regarding the Customer...I only wish Gandhi were still alive to read it.

"A Customer is a shared resource for both them and a Supplier. Having a customer means that we have a mutual agreement and partnership to supply a product and service to each other. The Customer needs us as badly as we need them; it is a relationship which needs to be kept in good standing. The common understanding between both the Customer and the Supplier should always be, *that the pleasure is all mine*...and when it's not, there should be a parting under friendly terms."

The most dangerous aspect for any Supplier Business is when the Customer(s) starts running your business.

Whenever your business decisions are based around what "The Customer" wants, then you have lost the independent sovereignty of your business ownership or company Quality Management System (QMS).

The specialty and uniqueness of your business gets badly compromised.

You should be able to sell your product(s) or service according to your ability to supply the demand, without concessions to a specific customer's business structure or their internal policies.

The problems begin when you cannot meet On-Time Delivery (OTD) schedule dates or you have Quality Issues with the product you're producing (Escapes and Returns).

It really becomes hurtful if you have only one or two customers or one large customer that makes up the majority of the Total Sales and Income of your business.

This is where the fear to compromise sets in.

The key indicator that you've lost control is when you have to start using the customers document formats for your own Process and Procedures and perform internal tasks according to their format and procedure for any Quality Functional Process...you're really screwed when that happens!

This will most likely infringe on and circumvent your approved internal QMS and ISO/AS Registrar approval, unless you are willing to go all the way and rewrite your Quality System and Procedures, then conduct the required Internal Audits to that new System.

Man, that's a lot of work!

Hope you can keep that customer for awhile and can make up for the lost time and profits in the meantime.

All too often the businesses that have the "Going out of Business" or "For Lease" sign in the window is not due to bad market share or the economy dropping off or even losing your customer base.

In all honesty it's the bad business decisions and practices of the business or company to not have a contingency plan to live within their means or regroup and recover.

It's the same old strategy to ignore the losses due to bad business decisions, keep wasting time and resources pleasing a bad customer, try to keep the profit margins within the projected estimates by layoffs and reductions in resources, work a lot of overtime (including holidays and weekends) and reduce the benefits to compensate for the losses.

More than anything, the mindset should move away from only satisfying the Customer and dump the negative financials and losses due to the Bad Customer(s); and recoup to make some kind of profit for the year, even if it doesn't meet the forecast projected. Think like you want to keep your business in business by taking on the challenge and believe that,

"Quality is Everything!"

WALSTON RULE #8

"It's Peace through Strength,
not the other way round"

In this chapter, we're going to view the effects on Quality from a social-political perspective.

Where the effects of governments ruling societies shapes the social, economic and Quality of lifestyles within the diversity of Freedom and Oppression.

The early 1950's saw the world entering into the threshold of a different kind of political tyranny.

A new mindset for every person born-to the so-called Freedom of Democracy on the right and the Iron Hand of Marxist Communism on the left.

The "Cold War" was ushered in by the onset of the Atomic Age.

After World War II, the Union of Soviet Socialistic Republics (USSR) obtained a quarter of the world's power and soon after that China would reach those ranks as well.

Together with the technology to manufacture and deploy an intercontinental nuclear warhead, they put themselves in the status of a superpower, next to the United States.

Very quickly, there was a noticeable divide between free nations in Europe and territories which were once sovereign countries with independent governments, that Russia was gobbling up into States forming the USSR.

The Military Alliance of nations in Europe formed after WWII under the guidance and leadership of the United States, called the North Atlantic Treaty Organization (NATO), set up defense and tactical bases with full scale military support personnel and resources against what was now identified as a formidable enemy.

The USSR was quickly viewed by the free world as the "Dark Empire".

Their oppression was a remnant of Russia's early history when the Czar's ruled, yet Marxism had given them the misconception of commonwealth unity but without the freedom of democratic representation.

China on the other hand was overpopulated, backward in their national infrastructure with technology and shrouded in mystery and poverty.

They were concentrating their resources in building up their military and proudly demonstrating their Communism as the Red Chinese in cohesion with the USSR.

A ruthless tyrannical dictatorship who paralleled the Russians in every evil cause behind every radical purpose to spread Communism world-wide.

On a global scale these forms of government became a cancer which had to be stopped, but the threat of nuclear annihilation altered the traditional military thinking on full-scale warfare.

From then on, it was diplomacy and a show of force through stockpiling nuclear arsenals.

An entire generation would be born and raised in fear of a "Doomsday Device".

Forevermore, mankind could, at the press of a button and a moments notice, leave us with a burning future and no escape from the coldness of a Nuclear Winter and the remains of degenerate mutations, once called *Homo Sapiens*.

Because no one wanted to use the term "war" to identify any military intervention, the term "Conflict" became politically acceptable.

That compromise led the United States into two future theaters of Conflicts which ended in anything but victory, with staggering loss of life and demeanor of national pride.

Korea and Vietnam were both about fighting the Cold War with China and the Soviet Union on their terms.

In the author's opinion, having been a Vietnam Veteran and my father a Korean War Veteran, I don't believe that the United States Government ever intended to win a final outcome to these Conflicts.

It wasn't about fighting an enemy who was directly threatening the homeland or had the approval of the majority of the American population to be viewed as that.

These were battles over invested interests, both political and corporate, and lining the pockets of individuals who wanted the fight but would never go themselves.

There was no "American" consensus to go to War, just patriots with their sense of duty, honor, and love for their country the _United States of America_, who got drafted into it!

The Kings of the East (China / Asia) and the Bear of the North (Russia) as referred to by ancient Scriptures, have been two Dark Political Forces on this planet.

Combined, behind the censorship of the Iron Curtain and away from the scrutiny and reporting of a Free Press, they've murdered millions of their own population to impose, enforce and spread the political tyranny of Communism in their own countries and throughout the world in a meager span of fifty years.

Three generations currently alive today have witnessed these atrocities and like myself, my father and millions of others who were called upon and took up the banner of Freedom to serve and fight against what we believed to be an evil oppression, which to this very day wants nothing more than complete world dominance and control of our Liberty.

The New World Order is nothing more than a new attempt from the same old dictatorship handbooks of the former Soviet Union and Chinese Communists for World domination under their political and social agendas.

The United States and the other Free World nations should not think for a moment that Russia and China are embracing capitalism or democracy just because the Russian flag became Red, White, and Blue after we supposedly bankrupted them and ended the "Cold War".

And don't think China is either just because they like McDonalds and Disney, we still import more goods from them than they will ever from us.

What the 45th and 47th President of the United States, Donald Trump, was doing with increasing Tariffs with China goods, is putting the USA at an even keel with our long-term Trade Deficit which we have created over the last forty years.

Their Million-Man [Plus] Army needs money and resources to run that huge machine and that's just what we're supplying them with as we pig out on their cheap crap every day from Walmart, COSCO, the 99 Cent Store and so many others.

Their ideology is not Strength through Peace, Peace is the last thing on their future agendas.

Their world dominant theology projects them into a warring mentality and conqueror syndrome.

The United States should be very careful never to project a retaliatory conflict against these powers as they flex their warring tactics and try to bring us into battle first.

The Giant Bear, rising up on its hind legs, bellowing out frightful roars and making gestures of attacking; and the Dragon spewing out fire from its mouth and wiping its huge tail, consuming the masses in its path.

These two superpowers are the epitome of evil and the enemies of Freedom and Liberty. They support every rogue ideology and dictator in the world and fight the United States at every opportunity to suppress Freedom and Democracy by supporting the infrastructure of the world's dictatorships.

There is no reprieve to Freedom as we embrace it here in the United States by any Socialist or Communistic entity; and no banner waiving of the Freedom and Rights as we commonly uphold them in the United States or anywhere else in the entire world!

Civil Rights, Human Rights, Freedom of Speech, Freedom of Rights to Life, Liberty and the Pursuit of Happiness started with the United States of America and remains only because of the existence of this country and our Value System of Freedom and Liberty.

The oppressive and sinful nature of mankind is inherent within all the Human Race, but the Inalienable Rights to which Freedom is attributed come from the Creator (God).

Unfortunately, these are constantly met with opposition and must be fought for and given sacrifice to by those who want Freedom more than oppression and slavery.

I see Quality the same way I see Freedom; as a "Good" thing.

Where the essence of Perfection meets the ability to get there.

To strive for Quality is to want the "Very Best Of" and to fight for and maintain Freedom gives us the ability to exist in that environment.

Who in their right mind would want to purchase, use or live with "Bad" non-conforming product? or justifiably in their minds want to or choose to live under a dictatorship in an environment of slavery and oppression?

These are usually situations that you are born into, but whenever individuals have the opportunity to escape to Freedom, they take it, they fight for it...they even die for it!

The innate character within us all is to be Free and make choices which satisfy the desires of our hearts.

To prosper and enjoy life in a Quality way and have the ability and freedom to be all that you can or want to be, is the essence of the United States of America.

Even in poverty, if there is Freedom, you have Hope of Improvement and the resources are available in the surrounding environments to energize ways of betterment.

But without Freedom and under oppression and slavery, Hope is fleeting, and the resources are not available, nor the ability to improve beyond the poverty surrounding you.

As we came through that difficult economic situations of 2009 and faced the challenges which went beyond, equal opportunity and equality under the law were holding on for dear life in the United States. The same was true in just the last Administration (Biden) and we as a nation were in jeopardy of losing not only our financial liberties, but our moral and national lifestyle due to corruption and perversion.

Even now as this book is being written, we are being greatly attacked from within by political anarchists and treasonous tactics pushing Socialism and Communistic agendas and using that Manifesto as never before experienced in our nation's history.

In the author's opinion, this is not merely politics and the incestuous desires of political lunacy by the Left of the Political Spectrum; but rather a spiritual upheaval, trying to usher in a Force of Acceptance to a complete secular Socialist World Order and through a Marxist agenda.

One that strips individuality of Title and Wealth, of Free Enterprise, of Private Sector Ownership, of making Personal Choices and the taking away of our Freedom and Liberties.

The movement at hand is very heavy towards "Uni" (One World) alliance, One Party dominance, with accepting Diversity at any cost, forcing governmental controls and socialism on the Constitution of a Free and Sovereign Nation who, by the way, is the only Federal Republic dominated by a Free Enterprising Capitalist Democracy in the world.

The complete About-Face within the turn of this century has been our posturing in regard to a Defensive Strategy.

From the Revolutionary War through the "Cold War" era, the United States pretty much embraced the tough ideology of "Peace through Strength", which means having a strong, well trained, and well stocked military and not afraid to express it or use it.

Many of our Heroes and Presidential Hopefuls were military icons.

Only a few brief periods in our Presidential history, has a very liberal stance influenced our Defense Strategy away from a strong military presence and strength.

In trying to garner the first World Order through alliance and diplomacy for Peace rather than War, President Woodrow Wilson vanquished Europe after World War I by personally promoting a united forum called the League of Nations.

Wilson, viewed by liberals as the Father of the Progressive Movement, was the advocate of government running everything, including a World Order of Diplomats to unite, govern and negotiate a Banner of Peace and Social Order.

The idea was a roaring success and an overwhelming hit with the Europeans, considering their collective unity in military strength couldn't fight a wet noodle without the United States as a military ally, which helped win them their victory in WWI.

Had we not taken the charge and entered the War when we did, all of Europe would have been speaking German and under the feudal lordship of the Deutscher Kaiser.

Nevertheless, Wilson could not get the U.S. Congress to support his political dream of world unity and the United States never entered into alliance with the League of Nations.

The League did nothing to stop a second maniac from coming out of Germany fourteen years later, with a strong and even more determined agenda for world domination.

The strategy of *Going to the Negotiation Table* gives your enemy a foothold; it allows them to buy time to arm themselves and build a war machine beyond your capability under the shroud of political posturing for peace and the liberal hopefuls betting it will work.

Something like what Adolf Hitler did with British Prime Minister Chamberlin in 1938, when he walked away with a worthless signed piece of paper declaring Peace and then five months later Hitler started a full-scale attack and take-over maneuvers on Europe, which started the largest and (if we include the Holocaust of six million Jews) the bloodiest war in modern history.

Funny how history has a tendency of repeating itself, especially when there are no "Lessons Learned" and you make the same stupid mistakes as before.

So, we fought a Second World War with the same enemy in Europe from the first one, but this time we made sure they couldn't unite again after winning the war by dividing their territories up between the two major allies, the United States and the USSR.

The problem was that the United States who led and controlled the Ally Forces, didn't give much consideration to what kind of monster the Russian Communists and Stalin really were.

As Stalin began to blockade the eastern sector of Berlin and then spread the blockade (Iron Curtain) across Eastern Europe, no one could imagine what the next four decades would bring in suffering, oppression, and utter impoverishment for the people of the Union of Soviet Socialistic Republics.

We did the same thing in the Pacific Theater with Japan.

To appease and acknowledge the Chinese as contributors during our fight with Japan (who by the way was China's devout enemy), the Chinese allowed the United States territorial access within their boundaries to establish bases and safe zones for landing aircraft while attacking the Island Nation on strategic bomb runs.

The Cold War didn't just happen out of well-executed planning to let the Communists take over half the world; it was a bad Quality decision on the part of the United States to not understand what kind of threat this political and social power really was in regard to a Tyrannical Monster.

The breakdown was by not following a Quality Process for building the Strategic Planning to liberate Europe.

It was primarily a political appeasement and intimidation by Stalin as a third-party member of the Allies to avenge the Germans for trying to exterminate them.

The Russian Plan had all the earmarks of a good Quality Process.

They had a policy, mission and were working to a standard that accepted Zero Tolerance for Failures.

They also had a method for corrective actions with non-conformances; as a dictatorship, they would eliminate all opposition and scrap the results by censoring the information and media.

The agenda for world domination was always in the Communist Manifesto, even as they were pretending to be allies of the United States during WWII.

We were helping them fight their enemies (Germany and Japan).

Once the battle was won, Russia wasted no time to quickly demand the Eastern territory of Germany and moved to secure their borders around that area and close it off.

When the Big Three (Roosevelt, Churchill, and Stalin) Allied Forces of the European Theater met to divide the Power Distribution after the War, the United States caved towards Russia wanting so much.

Churchill had mentioned that Russia was a Force not to be reckoned with and that we may see then at another time under different circumstances...meaning, *In Battle*.

General George Patton warned General Eisenhower who was the Supreme Allied Commander of the Forces in the European Theater, to not allow Russia to have any power or land grab in Europe.

Patton had devised a war plan against Russia to immediately move against the Soviet's while we had our full Army strength still in Europe and take control of that region, moving it under American governance.

He warned Eisenhower that we would fight a war with Russia in the near future.

We were so consumed by what the Imperialists and Nazi's had just tried to do and the long, drawn-out war, that we did not foresee the danger of anything other than Democracy as being settled into the regions of occupied Europe and Asia.

Following the Post WWII Era, technology and science exploded into missile defense, satellites, computers, telecommunications, lasers and of course *Software*...basically all electronics.

Military and Aerospace Standards and Specifications would rule the free world Defense Industries for three decades and sometimes would fall into the hands of the not so free world Communists.

From our end, the United States would produce superior "Quality" product and design throughout the Cold War Era and into the turn of the 21st Century.

The Process Models, Methodologies and Ideologies of Quality would change as well; moving to assure the science behind the technology would not exceed its capabilities of producing the products to the design criteria and processes.

With each new product innovation, comes new process implementations and training of the workforce to that technology and methods of building.

The author chose both Socialism and Communism 'vs' Capitalistic Democracy in this chapter as comparisons because like Quality, there is a good and a bad level of acceptability; and like Quality, there is a quantifiable Value System that can be determined and measured.

Any comparison to our life's journey within the society we live or the Global attempt to bring us all under a single controlled power of political persuasion, can be compared to an established Quality System and the pretext of how a well-defined and executed QMS is imposed and successful.

One thing to always keep in mind; Quality should be a way of life, in every aspect of it, so that the outcome of each performing task can be achieved at maximum efficiency and with the freedom to exercise judgments and reconcile non-conformances to the satisfaction of Quality.

As we move into a more liberal political embracement for worldwide Peace, our defensive posture will vary greatly, but our goals and policies to produce the highest Quality Products and Services should not vary and always maintain that:

"Quality is Everything!"

WALSTON RULE #9

*"Change is usually the result of something
that needs improvement,
and the preemptive action thereof"*

If there is one universal word that usually gives the appearance of youthfulness and progression, it's "**Change**".

I've concluded that if you wanted to define what the intent of Change is, it is - *to make a difference by conversion, transformation, varying, mutating, amending, or altering something in a distinctly different form from what it was originally in appearance, but usually to preserve the identity.*

Change can occur on or with anything in existence; it is the one thing that is constantly occurring in the physical universe or natural state of our physical life.

Change is the first thing called for when something is no longer working or needs replacement; like if your job is stagnated and you need to Change your career path, or every time you take a shower you Change your underwear.

Change can have a good side or bad side to its circumstance; it can give the appearance of betterment and produce negative impact.

The energy it takes to impose the preemptive action of Change is usually greater than sustaining the existing condition; therefore, Change should always be well planned and viewed as a necessary improvement before being implemented.

Change for the sake of change is ludicrous.

To say, "We need to change the way we are doing business", doesn't necessarily require changing anything.

It could imply that the processes that have been put into place are not being used properly.

The Quality Improvement Process (QIP) is one method of evaluating whether change should be implemented.

QIP is a systematic approach to the aggregate reduction or elimination of waste, rework and cost of redundant activities.

Targeted under the LEAN-Six Sigma process approach, Quality Improvement forms the basis of the ISO/AS9100 Quality Management System.

The leading contributor and innovator to these processes was Dr. W. Edwards Deming who introduced Total Quality Management (TQM) and applied Statistical Process Control (SPC) methodologies into the manufacturing environment and opened a visual venue into the "Hidden Factory" areas in production manufacturing.

During the early to mid-1980s, Dr. Deming and his Team of consultants were a major contributor to the authors mentoring process and career path, building the foundation for this work, "Quality is Everything!",

Even though the new direction of the Quality Improvement Process and Quality Management System within the Aerospace Industry is based around the PDCA Cycle (Plan-Do-Check-Act), this too was developed by Dr. Deming through his Total Quality Management Model. It is something that the author embraces as the fixed model for any Quality System imposed in a Manufacturing Business Environment.

TQM is truly K.I.S.S.

Segueing into an important aspect of any business are many Quality Models to follow in building Quality infrastructure.

Nevertheless, the most commonly used and accepted is Total Quality Management (TQM),

The concept of TQM has been around since after World War I (WWI), but applied in the Aerospace and Automotive Industries since the late 1980's.

From a functional perspective it attempts to retain or regain competitiveness in order to achieve customer satisfaction and is especially attractive in the face of increasing competition from around the world in this era of globalization.

TQM is an integrative philosophy of management for continuously improving the quality of products and processes.

The core of its practicality is to embed Quality synonymously throughout all functional organizations and applications in the business.

The backbone of TQM is having Top Management driving the program and making sure the environment to ensure success has been created.

The Key Principles that drive TQM Model:

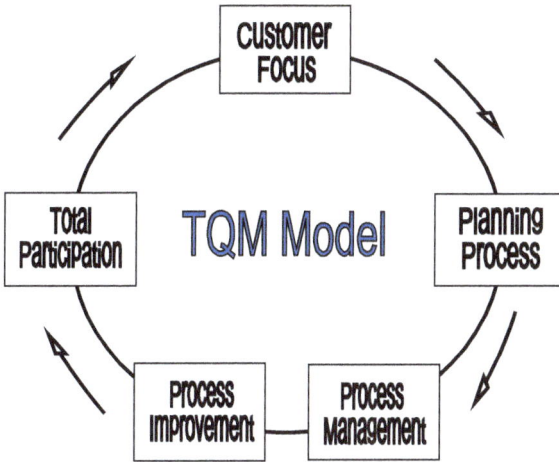

These inter-relate within key processes as cross-functional product design, process management, supplier quality management, customer involvement, information and feedback, committed leadership, strategic planning, cross-functional training, and employee involvement.

TQM has been the most successful Quality Model because it brings all of the functional organizations into a continuous cycle around each other, which forces discipline to interact on Continuous Improvement and utilizes the entire employee workforce to do so.

But I must say, that the political and institutional pressures from the Major Aircraft OEMs and ISO Globalists of the

Aerospace/Aviation Industry, have desired to make this model obsolete and turn a simple concept and perfect model into what is considered a dinosaur.

The concept of the PDCA Cycle (see Figure 9-1) is the international standard and idea of transforming TQM into a Globalist State of Control. It's a pattern that has been infiltrating the Aerospace Industry in the United States because of our desire to obtain more Globalization in our marketplace and increase profit beyond what we had previously ever considered possible. It's again that Greed has allowed us to compromise our Lead Position in this Industry and has allowed 3rd World and other foreign competitors an advantage over the Standards and Processes that we (USA) once held as World Dominance over.

Figure 9-1   PDCA Cycle

TQM is tracked around three (3) variances, which also provide the costing categories for identifying the price associated with non-conformances.

These are **Prevention**, **Appraisal** and **Failures** (Internal and External).

Prevention would be things planned before manufacturing began to anticipate areas of processes and functions that may lead to non-conformances such as: Design Reviews, Creating a Quality System, Creation of Plans for Quality, Reliability,

Operational, Production and Inspection, Training and Preparation and Maintenance of Processes.

Appraisal would be things associated with the vendors and customers evaluation of purchased materials and services to ensure they are within specification, such as: verification of incoming parts and materials to specifications, Quality Audits of processes, Supplier/Vendor assessments and approvals.

Failures are categorized as Internal and External.

These are identified as non-conformances through the MRB Systems and reported as Cost of Poor Quality.

Internal Failures are such things as: Wasted Time or Waiting time, Bad Inventory Control Techniques, Inspection Findings (Rejects), having to conduct MRB and Failure Analysis, Scrap, Rework and Repair.

External Failures are such things as: Field Repairs, Supplier Non-Conformities, Warranty Claims, Customer Complaints, Goods Damaged due to Bad Packaging and Returned.

TQM has a profound and powerful impact on managing your business to a Prevention proactive method rather than a Detection reactive method.

It doesn't matter how large or small the business is, TQM is a perfect fit due to its emphasis on Process.

Probably the first interactive Quality Model within a manufacturing environment with Inspection applications was Statistical Quality Control (SQC).

Introduced by Dr. W. Edwards Deming after World War II, SQC was based on the notion that a variation in the production process leads to variation in the End-Product. If the variation in the process could be removed this would lead to a higher level of quality in the End Product.

From this evolved Statistical Process Control (SPC) out of the Aerospace Industry in the 1960's.

The true power of SPC is in its ability to examine a process and the sources of variation in that process using tools that give weight to objective analysis over subjective opinions and that allow the strength of each source to be determined numerically.

Variations in a process may affect the Quality of the End-Item or Service.

SPC can give notice of these variations and reduce waste in both time and non-conformances which result in rework and scrap costs.

This usually leads to a reduction in the time required to produce the product or service from end to end and the cost savings associated with it.

Typical graphs and charts used for SPC are:

- Variable and attribute charts

- Average (X^-), Range (R), standard deviation (s), Shewhart, CuSum, combined Shewhart-CuSum, exponentially weighted moving average (EWMA)

- Process and machine capability analysis (C_p and C_{pk})

- Process characterization

- Variation reduction

- Histograms

- Cause and effect diagrams

SPC is not an adequate means of monitoring small flow-thru volumes of product.

It is best utilized in large volume capacity, fast-paced assembly-line or machine operator environments where the charts are displayed right on or next to the machine or assembly-line operation.

By these means, the performance and variations of the machine or assembly-line are manipulated according to the chart data or statistically running the process.

The most complex and detailed model used for improving manufacturing processes and eliminate defects is Six Sigma (6σ).

Six Sigma is a business management strategy originally developed by Motorola in 1986.

The term Six Sigma originated from terminology associated with statistical modeling of manufacturing processes.

A Six Sigma process is one in which 99.99966% of the products manufactured are statistically expected to be free of defects (3.4 defects per million).

The "Six Sigma Process" utilizes six standard deviations between the process mean and the nearest specification limit (see Figure 9-2).

In this analysis, which is based on the calculation method employed in process capability studies, practically no items will fail to meet specifications [Capability studies measure the number of standard deviations between the process mean (μ) and the nearest specification limit in sigma units].

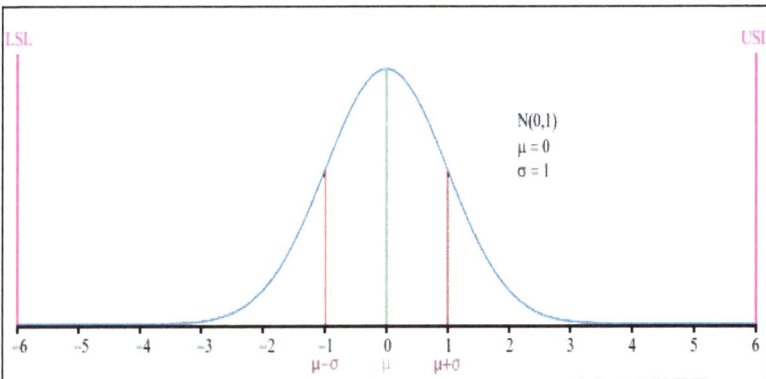

Figure 9-2 Six Sigma Normal Distribution

The advanced analysis tools and model reporting capabilities of Six Sigma make it superior to any Quality Improvement Method conceivable.

Some of the basic Management Tools (6σ) utilizes are:

- 5 Why Root Cause and Corrective Action
- Ishakawa Diagram (Fishbone Cause and Effect)
- Control Charts
- Failure Mode and Effect Analysis (FMEA)
- Pareto Charts
- Regression Analysis
- Taguchi Methods
- Pick Charts and Histograms

Sigma is based on different levels which are determined by a Process Capability Index (Cpk) and a Probability rate (DPMO) Defect Parts per Million Opportunity (see Figure 9-3).

Sigma level	DPMO	Percent defective	Percentage yield	Short-term C_{pk}	Long-term C_{pk}
1	691,462	69%	31%	0.33	–0.17
2	308,538	31%	69%	0.67	0.17
3	66,807	6.70%	93.30%	1	0.5
4	6,210	0.62%	99.38%	1.33	0.83
5	233	0.02%	99.98%	1.67	1.17
6	**3.4**	**0.00%**	**100.00%**	**2**	**1.5**
7	0.019	0.00%	100.00%	2.33	1.83

Figure 9-3 Six Sigma Levels with corresponding values

The standard Cpk for an existing process is 1.33 and on average, the normal process mean will shift by 1.5 sigma toward the side with the critical specification limit.

In this rule, less than and greater than Cpk (known as Short Term and Long Term Cpk), can be determined.

Six Sigma usually finds its application within the environment of Big Corporations who can afford the infrastructure and cost behind this endeavor.

It is not meant to replace SPC or the Quality Data System method of using a Data Acquisition and Trend Analysis System to report and identify the "Hidden Factory" non-conformance and reject rates.

It is the advanced approach of sustained continuous improvement which stands side by side with TQM and SPC.

As we entered into Computer Software technologies, engineering models such as the Capability Maturity Model (CMM) render process assessments and improvement methods which were only available to the Hardware Manufacturing arena.

Such tools are necessary in order to give data which disclose non-conformances and areas for Quality Improvement.

All non-conformances and areas of improvement lead to one bottom-line...COST!

The leading proponent of Change has to be with positive Improvement Strategies and the reduction of Cost.

One of the basic metric tools that Quality has available is known as Cost of Poor Quality (COPQ).

The COPQ should be reported at a minimum monthly in an easy-to-read graphic presentation with a front cover summary breakdown and Total COPQ Dollar Value and summaries concluding the total Cost in Dollar Values for each established data collection point.

The Report should include data from four (4) basic collection points:

1) Total Inspection Reject Rate (by Work Item Qty)

2) Total Defect Rate and Pareto (Total Items Inspected 'vs' Total Defects Found)

3) Total Supplier/Vendor Reject Rate (by Purchase Order Qty)

4) Total Material Review Board (MRB) Category Reject Rates:

    a) Rework / Repair

    b) Return to Vendor

    c) Scrap

The metrics for these are standardized and should reflect simple percentage values (see Figure 9-4a/b)

There must also be a dollar value attributed to each of the items in each of the four data collection categories listed above and percentages associated with the Reject to Build Ratio and Cost to Total Quantity Inspected.

A Non-Conforming Material Cost Summary should also be part of the COPQ Report to give a final summarized statement to close the report with. (See Figure 9-5).

If there is any better use for metrics and graphic presentations or displays, the Cost of Poor Quality should be at the Top of the List.

If collected properly and with full disclosure, the COPQ will provide the majority of the "Hidden Factory" and give the indicators that point to the Quality Improvements necessary.

Part of the Total COPQ should include within the figuring of MRB, the cost associated with the Board convening; the total personnel and time by an average hourly dollar rate, plus an average cost associated to each Inspection Non-conformance document written to identify the items presented in the MRB.

On average, the cost of generating the Inspection Documentation and disposition through the MRB Process is $250.

You must add this average cost, times the total quantity of Inspection Documents presented each month through the

MRB to get the administrative cost of the MRB, then you segregate the Scrap, Rework, RTV and UAI costs separately and add these all together for the Total MRB Cost.

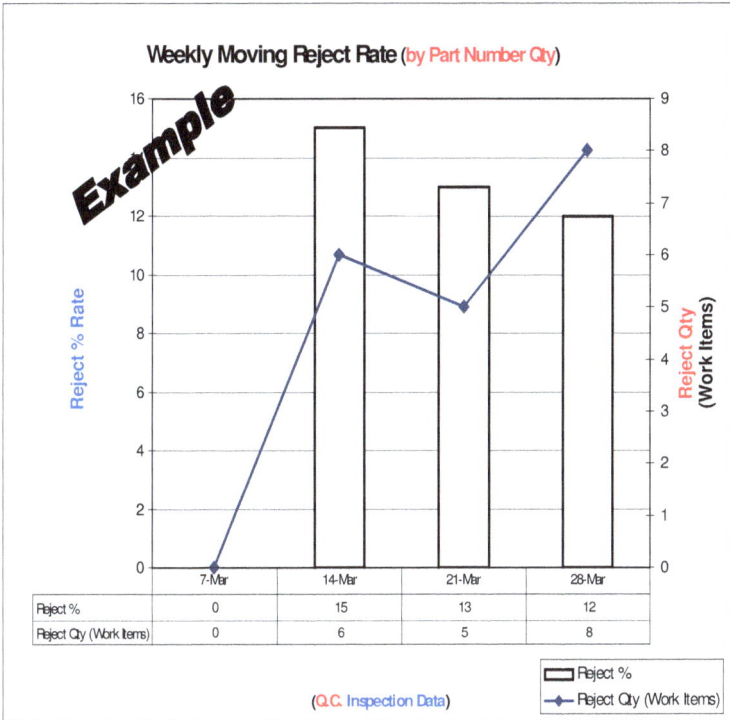

Weekly Moving Reject Rate (by Part Number Qty)

	7-Mar	14-Mar	21-Mar	28-Mar
Reject %	0	15	13	12
Reject Qty (Work Items)	0	6	5	8

(Q.C. Inspection Data)

Reject %
Reject Qty (Work Items)

Figure 9-4a COPQ Reject Rate

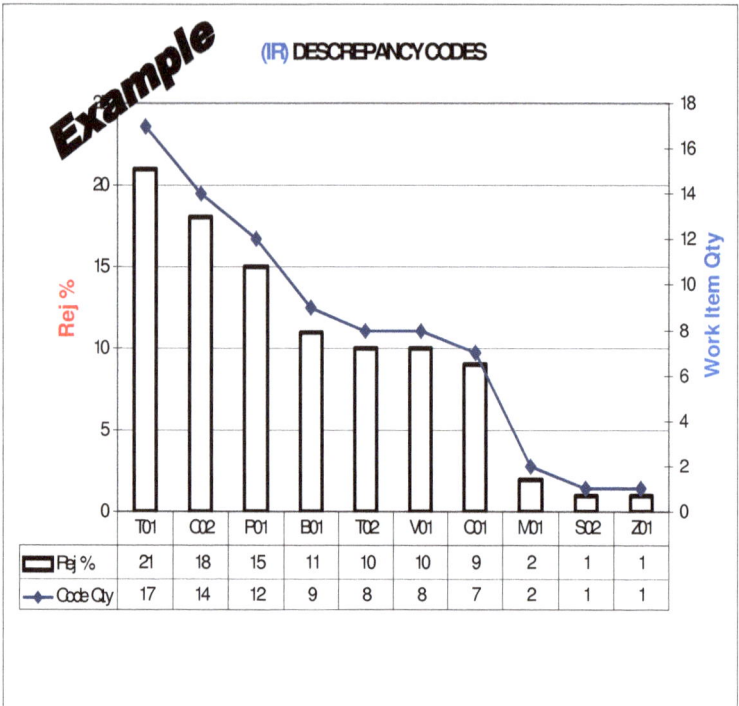

(IR) DISCREPANCY CODES

Example

	T01	C02	P01	B01	T02	V01	C01	M01	S02	Z01
☐ Rej %	21	18	15	11	10	10	9	2	1	1
◆ Code Qty	17	14	12	9	8	8	7	2	1	1

DISCREPANCY CODES

B01	–	WRONG DWG REV. BUILD
C01	–	FAILED PART / COMPONENT /TEST
C02	–	DAMAGED PART / COMPONENT
P01	–	WORKMANSHIP (INTERNAL)
M01	–	MISC
S02	–	PAINT ANOMALY
T01	–	SIZE / OUT OF SPEC / DIMENSIONAL
T02	–	NOT TO PRINT / SPEC
V01	–	VENDOR WORKMANSHIP
Z01	–	WORK ORDER / P.O. INVENTORY DISCREPANCY

Figure 9-4b COPQ Pareto Metric Graph

126

Non-Conforming Material Cost Summary

Month- March

Total (IR) Count= **58**

Total Qty Inspected= **35,883** ($138,443)

Total Defect Qty= **5,393** ($20,758)
(From ALL Process Work Areas)

Total Work Item Rejects = **913** ($14,500)
(Processed through MRB)

Total COPQ (4 Wks)= **$35,258**

	Total Defects QTY	Reject % From Total Process	Cost %	Total $
WIP				
Operations	4,530	84%	45%	$9,341
Stock/Inventory	658	12%	7%	$1,453
R/I	53	1%	20%	$4,151
Final/Ship	0	0%	0	$0
Test	0	0%	0	$0
Field Returns	2	0%	3%	$623
Vendor Related	150	3%	25%	$5,190
Total WIP/Supplier COPQ	5393	15%	25%	$20,758

	Total Defects QTY	Reject % From Total Process	Cost %	Total $
MRB				
Scrap	162	3%	2%	$624
Rework	3020	56%	33%	$11,624
Return to Vendor	593	11%	6%	$2,283
Use As Is (UAI)	1618	30%	18%	$6,227

	Total Qty	Work Item Qty	Cost %	Total $
Process (IR)s	58	913	41%	$14,500
			Total MRB COPQ	$35,258
			% of Total Inspection	25%

Figure 9-5 COPQ Non-Conforming Cost Summary

What I've suggested in Figure 9-4(a)(b) and 9-5 are very simple examples of a COPQ reporting scheme; the type of report is based solely on the complexity of your business model imagery and what you have established with clients or customers.

I have seen in the private business sector COPQ reports that look like something out of a Wall Street Financial Statement; with the DoD/Aerospace type business, they are very simple and styled in the manner of the examples (Figures) shown herein.

One final aspect behind reporting COPQ in a Production Manufacturing (WIP) environment is to bring into view the First Pass Yield condition.

This is where you show the values of non-conformance and acceptability.

It further shows correlation between the Work-In-Process flow by utilizing the Product Quality Indicator data points and the cost incurred with each point, to the final Inspection Buy-Off and Acceptance of each finished product.

Each PQI is a First Pass Yield indicator and the Cost for each of these Indicators (Points) can be collected, with the accumulated value being the reportable Work-In-Process COPQ.

So, the First Pass Yield is the amount and condition of all product being passed through PQI for the first time and being found to be "Build to Print" (Acceptable).

If the part is found to be rejected or failed in testing, then it is not counted as a First Pass Yield and if in the MRB the part is found to be acceptable or is disposition as "Use As Is", it can not be included in the respective PQI First Pass Yield count.

MRB has incurred additional, non-value-added cost and is included as part of the COPQ-FPY (Figure 9-6).

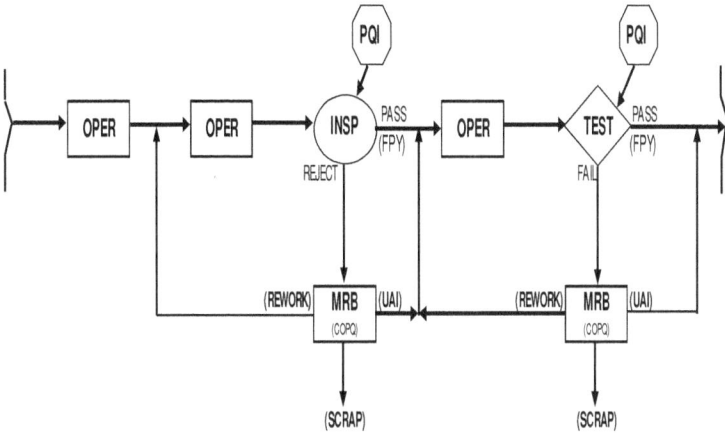

Figure 9-6   COPQ – First Pass Yield Functional Flow

*   *   *   *

As stated before, change for the sake of change is ludicrous.

The most existential example of all our country's history is how the American people blindly bought into a whole Presidential Campaign solely based on nothing but the propaganda of Change and "Yes We Can!".

Barack Hussein Obama III, played us with the intent of Change and a lot of free stuff for lower income and minority communities, using them as a political tool in getting elected President of the United States and it worked like a charm.

The hyped propaganda and use of superstar staging his appearances made it seem at times that something other than a mortal man was speaking at the podium.

The problem in doing that for his party constituents and the American People as a whole is the condition of Hope that Change promises is false and totally self gratifying.

He had a different agenda in mind once he became President than what he was expressing as Candidate Obama.

Given under a campaign banner, the topics of Change hit an accord, but the specifics are never completely known.

The Change Strategies and Implementation Plan are based on fulfillment after one is elected to the office and not before, so it is impossible to forecast the outcome of success ahead of time; so, the promise of Change is at best...Wishful.

When does Hope transform into Action and then Outcome?

All things in life boil down to either success or failure, satisfaction or dislike, Quality or crap.

Judaism has a wonderful salutation which expresses a heartfelt thankfulness to the Creator for the greatest gift possible, l'chayim חי (To Life), which is the preponderance of Chai (Living).

The expression is unique in that it does not characterize the Quality of Life but sanctifies life as the highest order of Joy and the expression of Hope.

The secondary mindset behind this would be dealing with the variations and levels of personal acceptance (Goodness and Well Being) verses dissatisfactions (Pain and Grievance).

Change should always bring about a positive outcome and incorporate Quality processes which assure success.

Quantitative results depend on the variations influencing the implementation activities: to every action there is a positive and equal reaction.

So, if an action is perceived as being "Good", then the supposition is a positive and equal "Good" reaction; thus, if an action is perceived as "Bad", then the supposition is a positive and equal "Bad" reaction.

Again, change for the sake of change is ludicrous; it should also be wanted.

The old adage, "If it's not broken, don't fix it!" has a lot of wisdom behind it.

Nevertheless, Progressive Thinking sees stable and consistent manner as stagnant and "Old Fashioned".

The youthful approach is "Out with the Old and in with the New".

In that mindset constant influx and rotation sets the order for revolution and Change becomes mandatory, whether you want it or not.

Whether it's needed, wanted or dictated, change in and of itself is a necessity in order to expand the venue of our human existence (Social, Political or Physical) and to keep up with the environment, or should I say, "*Changing Environment*" we live in.

We will not be successful in our quest for Quality if Change is a mandatory requirement; but rather if Change motivates, stimulates, and mandates that:

"Quality is Everything!"

WALSTON RULE #10
*"This is not a Democracy,
it's a Business"*

A job is not electing the boss you work for or the people you work with.

It's about performing a function that ensures, enhances, and supports the profit of the business which employs you.

It's not about me or them; it's about us.

Private business owners understand the concept of "US" a lot better than persons employed or employees of a company do.

The employee has a vested interest in themselves in most instances, while maintaining their employment for personal reasons.

Even if there is a Profit Share incentive between the employer and the employee, the vested interest is still with themselves and not the employer.

Whether it is a private business owner or a corporation with shareholders, the objective is the same; recoup investments, forecast and drive to the business plan, cut losses and make or exceed the forecasted profit margin.

With the employee, their mindset and focus are primarily on doing the job they were hired for and doing it to the best of their skill set, training and experience as much as possible and get a paycheck.

Career minded individuals may have a higher vantage point of this, as far as wanting to support the company's increased profitability, so they would be able to plan for retirement, but still the focus is primarily on themselves.

The insulting part for some people is when they get caught acting like a part-time employee, coming in late and leaving early doing the bare minimum.

You know the kind, not very motivated, just skating through the years of mundane and non-value-added existence, protected through some form of discrimination law like affirmative action, sex, age...whatever the state or federal legislative dreamers can think of to protect every working citizen (playing by the rules or otherwise), because the law is supposedly blind to discrimination.

The relative fact with these kinds of laws is that they greatly contribute to new forms of discrimination for the employers.

When management identifies these people as being *Slackers*, they suddenly come to life, loudly belching out justifications of their dedicated years of service and experience, which has so greatly contributed to making the company what it is...*Blah, Blah, Blah.*

These kinds of people, protected by liberal types of laws, which favor bad conduct and protect the offender and not the business, is why the H.R. Departments in most companies have doubled their staff in the last two or three decades, with a huge majority of their time and resource spent in lawsuits and litigation, instead of servicing the betterment of the company through Improvement Processes and increasing the skill set and training for the human development of their employees.

It is also the main contributor for many companies going out of business or losing their reputation.

The same and exact scenario exists in our education programs throughout the United States, from Kindergarten through High School Senior.

The emphasis is not placed on a Quality Education any longer and it has been going down that path since the mid to late 1970's.

It's all about ratio numbers, politics and political correctness in the workplace and the classroom; it's all about appearance and no substance which produces low Quality results.

The negative connotations of this are very real and we do have a very serious situation in America with increased dissatisfaction with employees and their jobs and employers trying to find qualified and lasting relationships with the people they hire.

The negative connotations are also very real within the American Public-School Systems, with decreasing test scores and scholastic attentiveness and we have seen a decline in the awarding of scholarships due to a lower pool of qualified candidates.

In order to meet any numbers within the scholarship awards, most regents had to lower the requirements in order to meet quota totals.

This means that the bar has been lowered once again, so the scholastics of these institutions don't fall behind in receiving awarded scholarships in equal opportunity manner, rather than an upper-level scholastic reward and risk public discrimination venue.

The essence should be that Quality is "Quality" and reflected at every level of business, society and life.

Remember as previously stated in this book, "Quality" is synonymous with expecting the "*Very Best of*" and is linked to a point of *Perfection*.

If compromised from this perspective, then the term, definition, philosophy, and application are worthless.

If you really want Quality in your business or even in your life, you must not compromise any portion of any process or activity which you have designated to be under Quality Control...meaning implement a Zero Tolerance to defects and non-conformances (expecting the "*Very Best of*") and Discipline yourself against Quality Work-Around (link to a point of *Perfection)*.

Compromise is the Enemy of any Quality Program, Process or Implementation Plan.

It might be the method of choice as part of a political process or negotiation format, but it has destructive characteristics when trying to counter-balance non-conformances and instill Quality Improvement Paradigm's.

The applications and methods of implementing Quality in your daily life and most importantly, at the workplace are essential in maintaining *Consistency of Flow* and *Reliability*.

Adopting a regiment of discipline and well-trained personnel is foremost in achieving any Quality Program successfully.

The discipline must be taken personally with each individual in the organization(s) and well written procedures and instructions thoroughly implemented through a robust training program, with documented evidence of each person participating.

This kind of accountability at the individual level is what renders group consensus and action to perform and maintain the business goals, policies and objectives towards Quality and profitability.

Dictating how a business runs is (or at least should be) management's responsibility.

Contrary to the stakeholder's belief that "the employees should have a say-so in running the business"; when it comes to making the decisions and directing the policies and authority, Management should be doing that.

It is important that management be sensitive to the workforce awareness of the "Hidden Factory" and latent anomalies within their respective processes.

A lot of Legacy builds up within departments where there is little movement of personnel or long-term employment.

Management should be taking the pulse from within their respective functional organizations and report it up the Chain of Command.

Mainly for visibility into Quality Improvements which, hopefully, is presented through an established Preventative Action Board (PAB) and robust Continuous Improvement Program.

It is absolutely essential that the Senior Management "Leadership" Team conduct regularly scheduled Quality Management Reviews and that the Quality Management

Representative present the State of Quality in quarterly segments and a final "End of the Year" Review Summary.

Above all things, a business survives by making a profit.

That's what is left over after expending the overhead: [utilities, rent, payroll (salaries, overtime and bonuses), benefits (paid time off, holidays, sick days, vacations, insurance, 401K matching), product material cost, consultants, vendors/suppliers, office supplies, city/state/federal taxes and regulatory fees, legal services, and <u>Cost of Poor Quality</u> (rework, scrap, warranty)].

Most employees think that overhead is the big, bloated salaries and bonuses management get, not realizing that the number one biggest Cost Waster is <u>COPQ</u> and having low First Pass Yield Rates from the manufacturing line and supplier deliveries…it's in their own backyard!

Management has a responsibility to keep ALL of the workforce informed on the State of the Business, from Top Management down to the person that collects the trash for recycling.

Letting everyone know the truth about the business and its affairs is a good thing so that people can be motivated to support and improve the areas that need help, because it's their business as well.

If there is one outstanding message in all of this, it should be that life on this planet is sustained by business and the flow of monetary reward for having one and being employed by one keeps us alive.

The customer base is fragile with any business.

Constantly being hounded by your competitors to attract people away from you to them, or rising costs and lack of sales, makes the challenge of owning and running a company nerve-racking at times.

If on top of it, you're also battling Quality issues which are repetitive and unstoppable, then you can literally hear that flushing sound of your profit going down the toilet every day.

When it gets painful enough, people usually stop and investigate where it's coming from and what is making it happen, so it can be stopped.

Only a fool keeps making the same mistakes with no sense of it.

The wisest and most competitive words that anyone could utter starts with a commitment to realize that Quality is more than an idea, more than a department and more than a system,

"Quality is Everything!"

CLOSING COMMENTARY
"Where we come from,
means more than where we are going"

This book is being written at a time in our history when a travesty is once again taking place in the United States, with worldwide affects and repercussions.

At a time when massive protests and underlying discourse is being manipulated by radical political and foreign powers, trying to break our government and Federal Republic apart. When we are at foreign Trade Wars with Tariffs on goods and services and outsourcing of goods from China, Mexico and India are constantly in question regarding Safety, Quality and Ethics.

All of this has contributed to weakening the U.S. dollar and elimination of career path opportunities in the American job market.

These are issues begging for answers but are falling on the deaf ears of a consumed public.

A time when the word "Cheap" is supposed to include the characteristics of Quality and the methods of marketing these products is so technologically advanced, with fantastic packaging and graphics, they give false visual affects and appeal which blinds the consumer in accepting Cheap as having the highest Quality attributes.

Then of course there's the price to be considered.

Cheaper Products in mass quantities cost less to produce and, in most instances, they are manufactured in countries where not only the material being used is of inferior Quality, but the manufacturing processes do not meet an agreed upon Quality standard.

"Made in America" has been the world standard for Products, Services and Quality since the Industrial Revolution took place at the turn of the 20th Century, but our new focus has moved towards Asia and our neighbours south of the border.

Corporate America (and in particular Wall Street) and the Labour Unions have slowly but consistently sabotaged the American workforce and our ability to produce goods and services by moving them to outsourced countries who do not either have our shared values or work force skill sets to produce Quality product...all of this in the name of Higher Profits and Shareholders Satisfaction.

The State and Federal governments have also done their share of the sabotage by adding more and more taxes to businesses, using them as a source of revenue to help balance their budgets and make up for bad political decisions and overspending tactics.

What these outsourced countries can do better than us is produce massive quantities of stuff at very low prices, very quickly.

Their biggest commodity available to them in doing this is a seemingly endless supply of human resources.

With the workforce utilized to make these products being numbered in the hundreds of millions and unemployment in very high and consistent percentages (40%-60%) and in too many instances includes either slave labour or child labour, where the average worker is making the equivalent of four to ten U.S Dollars a day, then Cheap should have a whole new meaning to the average American consumer.

In the name of humanity, where are the cries from all the activist groups in America?

You know, the ones who risk life and limb trying to sabotage whaling ships in international waters, or try to block the shipment from oil tankers in the San Francisco harbour, or the ones who call ICE and our Border Patrol Law Enforcement "Baby Killers", or the ones willing to live in trees for a year to protest protecting a species, or get court orders to stop using water to irrigate crops in the San Joaquin Valley because of a fish that used to spawn in the river, but doesn't exist any longer (don't want to kill any of the non-existent fish in watering food crops for humans) .

Oh, and where are all those college and university student protestors and activists and women feminists who so boldly speak out against violations of Human Rights in the United States? And what about the Children Rights Activists?

Why are they not protesting these goods which are being produced with the sweat and labour of children as young as nine years old from China, India, and other 3rd World Countries?

It's so ironic that even with the awareness of such atrocities taking place in the manufacturing of these products, we have become so greedy and insensitive to what good Quality is, we turn a deaf ear and blind eye to ignore it just so we can keep the endless flow of barges, with what we consider affordable products, coming to us from abroad.

As long as when we walk into Cosco or Walmart or Target or Best Buy or any of the many discount stores and the shelves are stocked to the brim, then life is good.

America is too caught up in the liberal agenda of being politically correct and making sure we do not offend the world (global) communities, no matter how offensive it is to our health, safety, national security, economy or ethics.

We turn a lie into the truth and visually propaganda it into every household, classroom, magazine, billboard and media venue.

The really sad part behind the propaganda push is that our own American advertising agencies pump hundreds of millions of dollars into the advertisement agenda to brainwash and actually change our society and culture away from demanding the highest Quality for products and services to demanding the cheapest cost and greater volume.

And oh, let's not forget the largest and most dangerous advocates of all this propaganda, our Fake News Liberal Media sources (CNN, MSNBC, ABC, CBS, New York and LA Times, etc).

The problem with the Cheapest Cost is that it usually equates with the Cheapest Quality.

There used to be a great American saying, "There is no free lunch".

Well, there is, but it's cheap, inedible, and very comparable to what we are getting in goods and services from foreign outsourcing and distribution: Cheap, unreliable and unsafe.

The analogy, "you can't put lipstick on that pig and make it attractive", is no longer true.

We do it every minute of every day with deceptive advertisement and propaganda.

The foreign Importers are the pig, and we supply an endless amount of the lipstick through propaganda resources.

Whatever happened to truthful and accurate advertising...or did that ever actually exist?

A few years back there was an alert by an American toy distributor that some of their toys made in China had lead in the paint and that babies were putting these toys in their mouths and getting sick.

After a few months of getting complaints from consumers the toy distributor issued a public alert and recall.

Lawsuits were pending with the American Toy Distributor, but only a handful of complaints were aimed at the factory in China who used the lead in the paint to begin with.

Those charges were quickly squelched by the State Department because it would have negative impact in our relations with China considering they do not do well with public criticism or "Losing Face".

We also have a little political problem with China in owning almost a trillion dollars of our national debt. No trump card there in our future, right?

We are blindly accepting the fact that a new paradigm has taken place in America without the general public having too much care about it and marching towards Change that has no real defined purpose except to join the masses towards socialized solidarity – Government run and supplied "Everything", this goes way beyond the "Big Brother" concept.

Since the second decade of the 20th century two main factions have greatly influenced political decisions in this country –

1) Banks and Wall Street.

2) Unions and Organized Crime.

Now we have the Drug Cartels and Illegal Immigration Trafficking Contraband and Human Resources to contend with an even higher rate of Crime Syndication.

Not that our elected representatives merely considered legislation based on lobbyists applying insight or pressure from these factions; but that these factions had them (our elected representatives and legislative process) in their back pockets.

We constantly accept the fact that the United States must be the leader in the Green Agenda or impose the strictest EPA laws in the world regarding the environment or hold an animals rights to every conceivable right of a human (*that is except the right of a baby to not be murdered in the womb*).

Why? Because we're the richest superpower nation in the world and have been told since post WWII that we need to be the example for the rest of the world to follow as well as the Policeman.

Well excuse my French, but *"C'est des conneries."*

The whole attempt and illusion behind Cheap Quality is to give the masses (the middle to lower class population), the ability to have what only the rich can afford.

Let's say for example, if you could get a thirty-five hundred-dollar Rolex look-alike for the price of a forty-nine-dollar Timex, wouldn't that be kind of a status thing to someone who couldn't afford the Real Deal.

When you hold the thing in your hand or put it on your wrist, from a distance it has the same appearance in design, colour and label as the Real Deal.

The difference of course, is in the hand-crafted workmanship, the precise Swiss Movement, superior materials being used, and that lifetime guarantee of Quality for those parts and labour, which is where the cost difference exists in the first place.

When Quantity of Substance supersedes the desire for Quality of the Product, you lose the art and skill of the Craftsman, striving for perfection and building Quality into every product as the mark of their reputation.

It is however replaced with the automated, mass produced, sweatshop worker being pushed by their Task Masters to produce so many parts per minute, TAKT time methodology or using a conveyer belt inspection process, doing fly-by visuals to grab the most obvious visual rejections, and thrown them into the scrap heap. Leaving of course, a built-in five percent reject rate due to human error.

What gets shipped and delivered is something that has the appearance of Quality but isn't.

What ends up becoming the mindset of the consumer is, *"so what if it breaks or wears out in a few months, it was so cheap I'll just buy another"* and the issue of Quality is replaced by convenience and cost.

I'm not sure America is completely out of the game with manufacturing hand-crafted Quality product or that the American public even cares about that any longer.

But one thing is for sure, we have lost our ability to compete in that arena because of our selfishness, laziness, and greedy desires to have more for less...and that is achieved through allowing foreign outsourcing what could be "Made in America".

We have been sold on the concept that Cheap is Quality and More is better, when in reality, what else can I say but,

"Quality is Everything!"

LASTWORD
by
George Rule CQE, CSQE

It is always a good feeling to have the *Last Word*.

It is especially so when the word follows a comprehensive, intelligent discourse on a subject so important and so passionately addressed. Yes, passionately. The author's mantra, that "**Q**uality is **E**verything", is not taken on lightly. He does not merely preach it. He lives it. I have learned to emulate this as his colleague and fellow Quality Professional. And now the mantra is shared by a thoroughly researched work pointing out the many venues and areas of life where the notion of Quality is seldom the driving force. The author points out that it should be and gives us the important "whys". Most importantly is the inclusion of some insightful "How's".

This work should help dispel some faulty, but widely held, notions of what "quality" is, and it serves to inspire some thought as to what it is not. It is not merely inspections after build. Nor is it recalls of defective products and the great expense incurred thereby. Quality, in all areas of endeavor, starts at the beginning, continues through process, and provides imprimatur to the end. So, what to do? The application of the Quality Science is the means. It saves time, money, and lives. It can be applied to products, process, finance, conduct of business, and conduct of our personal lives. This involves avoiding short sightedness in any endeavor. Simply stated, it involves the use of some common sense, as the author so thoroughly advises.

This notion of the Quality Science as common sense deserves some further discussion. One needs not be a scientist, Quality Engineer, or statistical whiz to apply it. But knowing a bit about the developers of this science and its application is helpful. We can, so to speak, stand on the shoulders of the Quality gurus of recent decades and arrive at good results through common sense application of what they have given us. This is what our author has taken great pains to point out in this work.

The works and tools of the great quality scientists are well known in the business and government realms. One would hope that they were more closely emulated. They have furnished wonderful tools for quality application in all areas of endeavor. Names like Shewhart, Deming, Juran, and Crosby are legend. And as Deming advised in lectures, these are simple and common sensical. They include control charts, invented by Shewhart and taught to Deming and Juran, to detect process problems in their infancy and to apply correction before quality is compromised.

They abhor the assessment of blame to workers. Application of common sense is incumbent upon management. That means top management, with follow-through to all involved. And their efficacy is well proven. Dr. Deming went to Japan after the Second World War and taught these to that nation. It resulted in a great leap of quality in Japanese products. But the lesson is that that these things must be valued and maintained. Recent lapses in application due to perceived "expense" or time constraints have resulted in expensive recalls of that nation's automobile products, greater costs of repair and recall, and possibly the immeasurable costs of lost lives. Japan is not the only example. Others serve to educate. Some large oil companies of Brazil, Britain, and the United States have caused great havoc by not observing these tools and lessons. While the protections provided for quality and safety were in place, they were often neglected with well-known tragic results. Mr. Walston's work provides a running analysis of how to avoid such pitfalls in events both great and small.

A great problem with applying Quality is the misperception that it is too expensive to implement and maintain, thereby adding to the time and cost of arriving at the final product, process, or law. Product and process quality become compromised in the name of "efficiency". This is a management fault. It is not a worker's fault. In fact, the exact opposite is true. When time and effort are taken to do things right from the beginning, with quality tools in place and observed, time, money, jobs, and lives are preserved.

So how does common sense apply? How does it matter to me? What can I do?

One way is to follow the advice of the greats. Juran defined quality in his many works simply as "fitness for use". So just check it out. Will it do what I want it to do without breaking?

Is it cheap? Too light? Too heavy? If so, beware. Is it warranted without laborious caveats? If not, beware. Is the fine print extensive? If so, beware. These things too often point to neglect of quality in the production of one's purchase, be it purchase of product, service, or anything else.

These are caveats brought out by our author in this work.

So, the *Last Word* must say something meaningful to all of us in obtaining that which indeed demonstrates "fitness for use".

And it can be phrased no more simply than:

"Quality is Everything!"

APPENDIX A

Walston & Associates

"Quality is Everything!"
SURVEY QUESTIONNAIRE

Date:_____

1) **Gender:** (M)_____ (F)_____

2) **Age:** 21-30___ 31-40____ 41-50____ 51-60____ 61-70____

   71+____

3) **Annual Income:** N/A____ 20K-40K____ 41K-60K____ 61K-

   80K____ 81K-100K____ 101K-120K____ 121K-140K____

   141K-160K____ 161K-180K____ 181K-200K____ 201K+____

4) **Race (Cultural ID):** Asian American____ Hispanic American____

   African American____ Anglo American____ Native American____

   Hindu American____ Mid-Eastern American____

   Foreign National (Not Citizen)____

5) **Place of Birth (Country):** _____

6) **City Currently Living:** _____

7) When you purchase a product, what are the factors driving your decision   (Rate 1=Highest – 4=Lowest)

_____ Quality (Performance Rating / Name Brand)

_____ Price / Cost

_____Appearance (Packaging) / Status Symbol

_____ Advertisement / Coupon Item

8) How many times, on average, do you grocery shop per month

0___ 1___ 2___ 3___ 4___ 5___ 6___ 7___ 8___ 9___ 10___

11+___

9) How many automobiles have you purchased in the last 10 years

0___ 1___ 2___ 3___ 4___ 5___ 6___ 7+___

10) How would you rate yourself as a shopper (Pick only one)

_____ Thrifty

_____ Frugal

_____ Sensible

_____ Take Caution

_____ Don't Care

11) Is the term "Quality is Everything" an accurate statement for your life-style

_____ Yes   _____ No   _____ 50/50

12) Where do you do your average shopping at... and what percentage

A- Products

_____ Strip Malls _____%

_____ Galleries _____%

_____ Internet (On-Line) _____%

B- Groceries

_____ Major Supermarkets _____%

_____ Convenience Marts (7-11, 99 cent stores, corner markets, etc) _____%

_____ Home Delivery _____%

13) In the last 10 years, what types of automobiles have you chosen to purchase   (Check all that apply)

_____ Luxury   _____ Sports

_____ Economy   _____ Electric/Hybrid

_____ Mid-Size Sedan/Coup   _____Truck/SUV

_____ Electric/Hybrid

14) When making purchases, is your mindset on the Quality of the product or Cost of the product   (Choose Only One)

_____ Quality   _____ Cost

15) If someone (A Stranger) came up to you and asked for money, would you give it to them (Pick only One)

_____ YES, It's only money

_____ NO, begging is not earning what you receive

_____ YES, charity is always a good thing

_____ NO, they're all SCAM artists

16) Whether at home or eating out, do you keep the left-overs (Doggie Bag) for the next day

_____ YES, don't want to waste anything

_____ NO, I can't stand eating the same food twice

17) Give the percentage of time per month that you:

A- Eat-In (Cook at home)

_____0% _____10-20% _____30-40% _____50-60% _____70-80% _____90-100%

B- Eat-Out (Restaurants)

_____0% _____10-20% _____30-40% _____50-60% _____70-80% _____90-100%

18) After you purchase something and the clerk gives you your change, do you count it

_____ YES, always

_____ Only if I think they made a mistake

_____ NO, never

19) When you find that something you've purchased is defective or not to the Quality you expected, do you return it for a Replacement or Refund

_____ Yes, always

_____ Sometimes, depending on the item

_____ No, never

©2016-2017 Walston & Associates   ken@walstonassociates.com

APPENDIX B

Walston & Associates

"Quality is Everything!"
SURVEY RESULTS METRICS

Survey Question #1

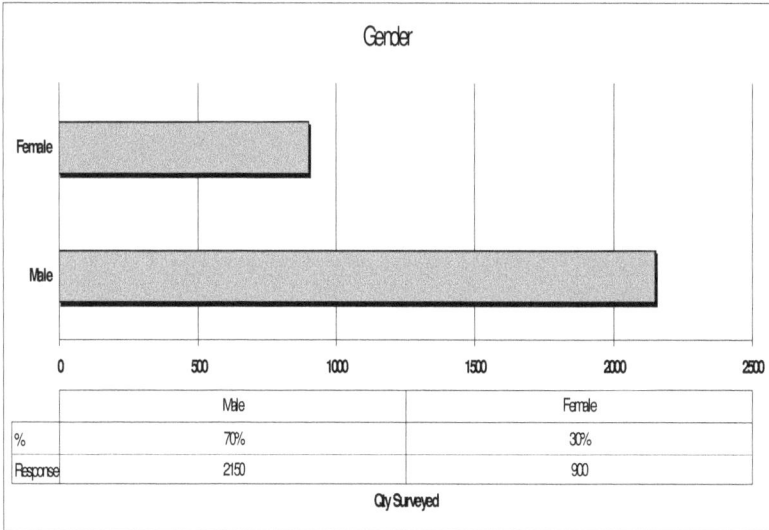

Gender

	Male	Female
%	70%	30%
Response	2150	900

Qty Surveyed

151

Survey Question #2

Age

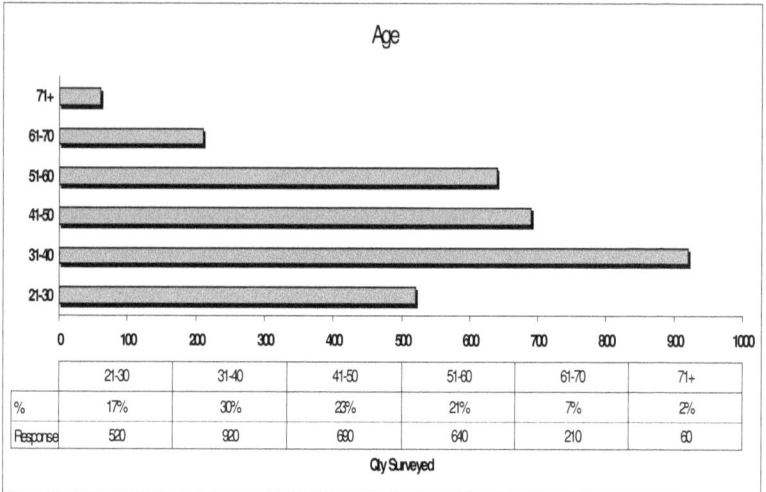

	21-30	31-40	41-50	51-60	61-70	71+
%	17%	30%	23%	21%	7%	2%
Response	520	920	690	640	210	60

Qty Surveyed

Survey Question #3

Annual Income

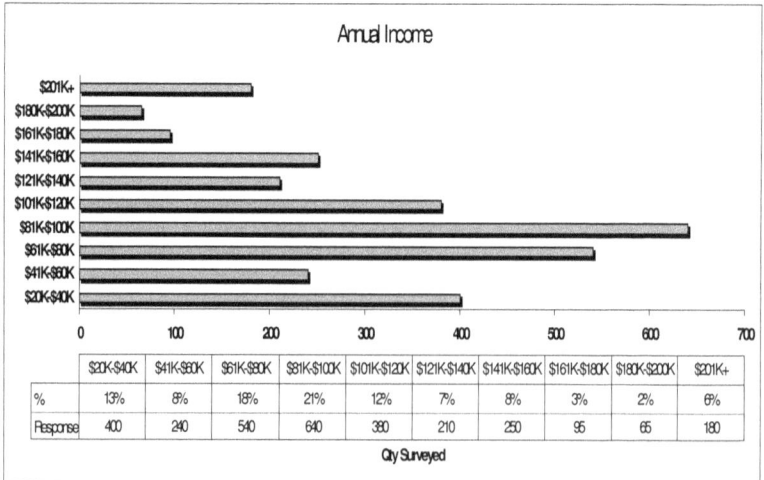

	$20K-$40K	$41K-$60K	$61K-$80K	$81K-$100K	$101K-$120K	$121K-$140K	$141K-$160K	$161K-$180K	$180K-$200K	$201K+
%	13%	8%	18%	21%	12%	7%	8%	3%	2%	6%
Response	400	240	540	640	380	210	250	95	65	180

Qty Surveyed

152

Survey Question #4

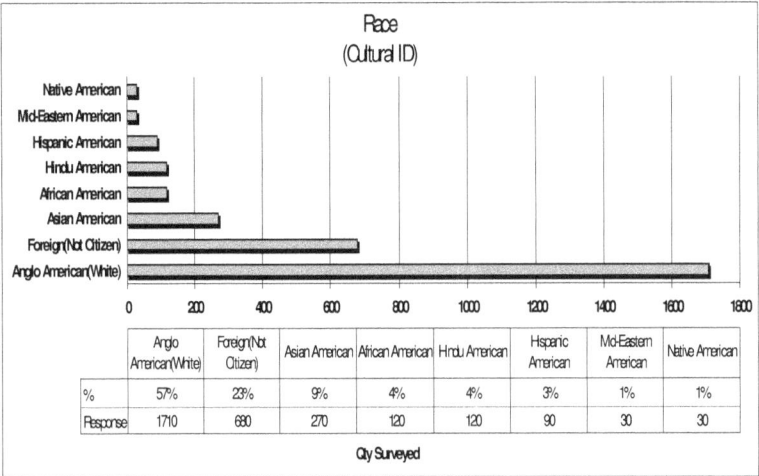

Race (Cultural ID)

Qty Surveyed

	Anglo American(White)	Foreign(Not Citizen)	Asian American	African American	Hindu American	Hispanic American	Mid-Eastern American	Native American
%	57%	23%	9%	4%	4%	3%	1%	1%
Response	1710	680	270	120	120	90	30	30

Survey Question #7

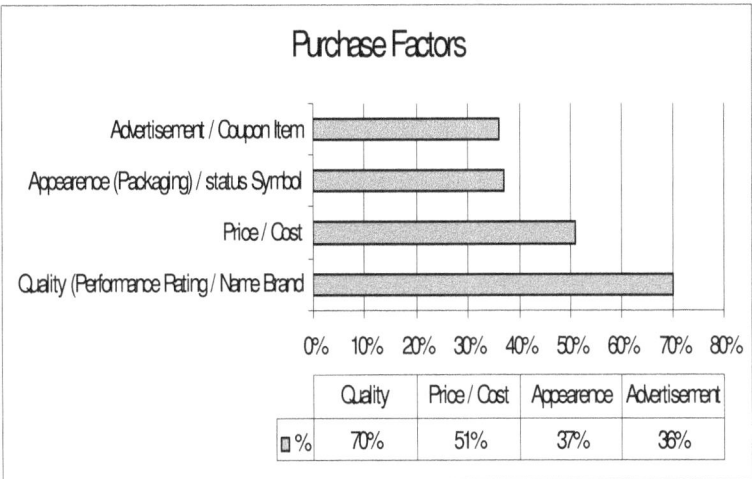

Purchase Factors

	Quality	Price / Cost	Appearence	Advertisement
%	70%	51%	37%	36%

153

Survey Question #8

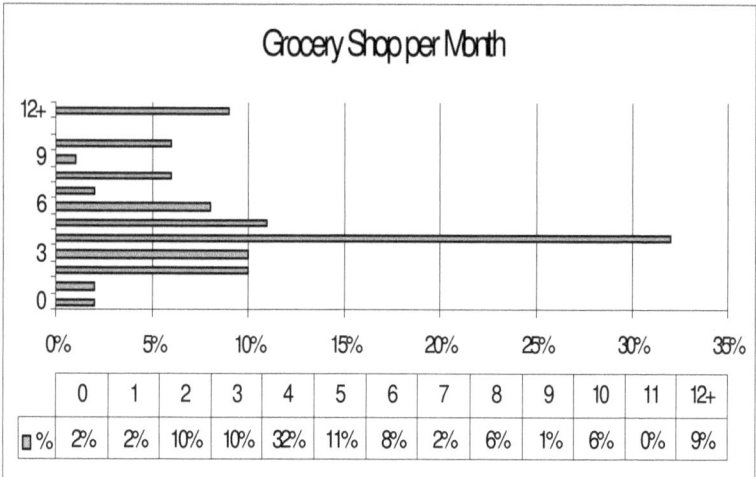

Grocery Shop per Month

	0	1	2	3	4	5	6	7	8	9	10	11	12+
%	2%	2%	10%	10%	32%	11%	8%	2%	6%	1%	6%	0%	9%

Survey Question #9

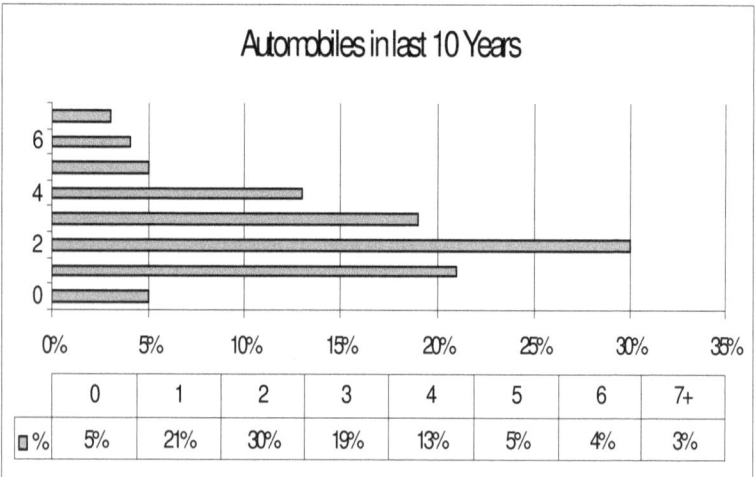

Automobiles in last 10 Years

	0	1	2	3	4	5	6	7+
%	5%	21%	30%	19%	13%	5%	4%	3%

Survey Question #10

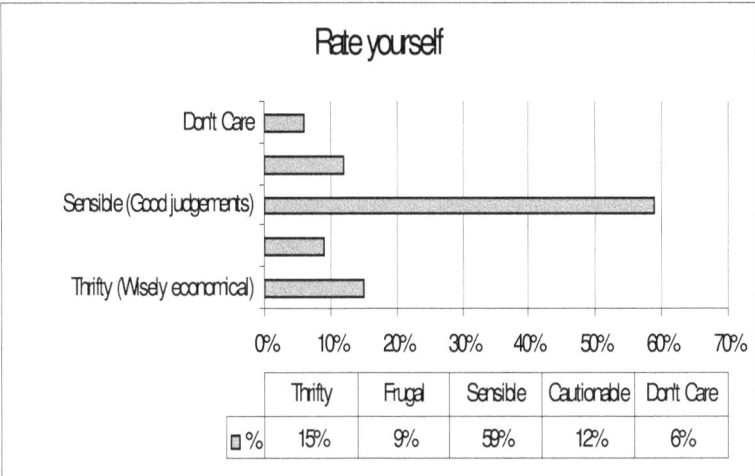

Rate yourself

	Thrifty	Frugal	Sensible	Cautionable	Don't Care
□ %	15%	9%	59%	12%	6%

Survey Question #11

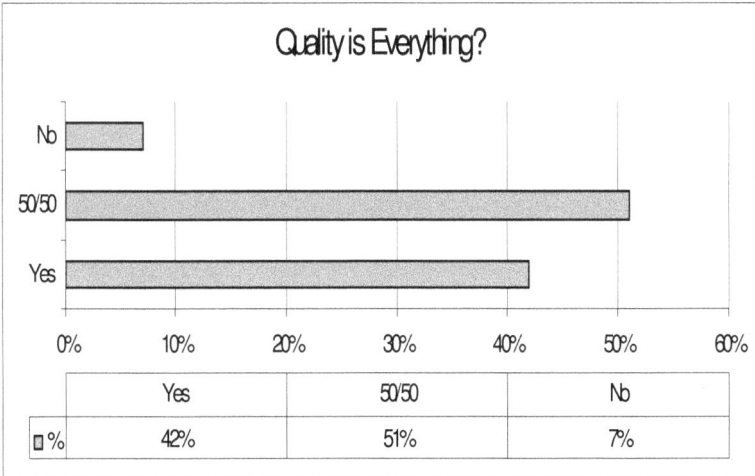

Quality is Everything?

	Yes	50/50	No
□ %	42%	51%	7%

Survey Question #12(A)

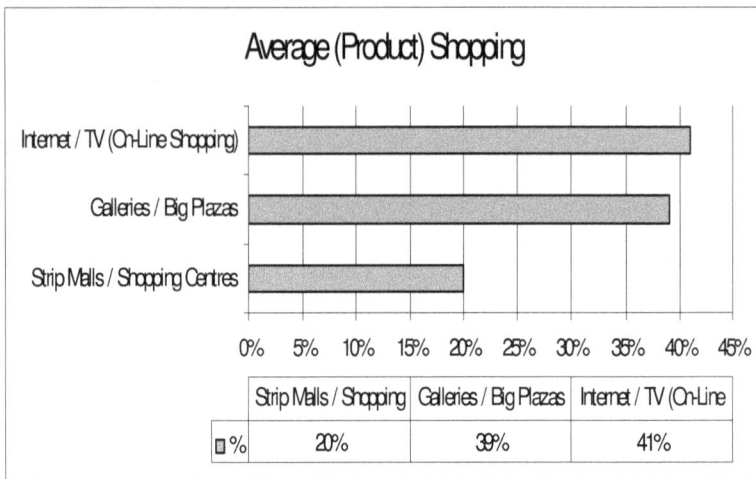

Average (Product) Shopping

Horizontal bar chart with categories:
- Internet / TV (On-Line Shopping)
- Galleries / Big Plazas
- Strip Malls / Shopping Centres

X-axis: 0%, 5%, 10%, 15%, 20%, 25%, 30%, 35%, 40%, 45%

	Strip Malls / Shopping	Galleries / Big Plazas	Internet / TV (On-Line
■ %	20%	39%	41%

Survey Question #12(B)

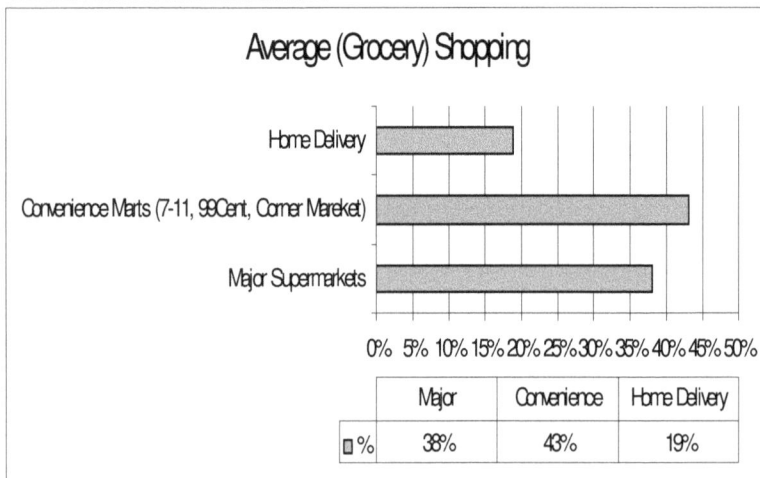

Average (Grocery) Shopping

Horizontal bar chart with categories:
- Home Delivery
- Convenience Marts (7-11, 99Cent, Corner Mareket)
- Major Supermarkets

X-axis: 0%, 5%, 10%, 15%, 20%, 25%, 30%, 35%, 40%, 45%, 50%

	Major	Convenience	Home Delivery
■ %	38%	43%	19%

Survey Question #13

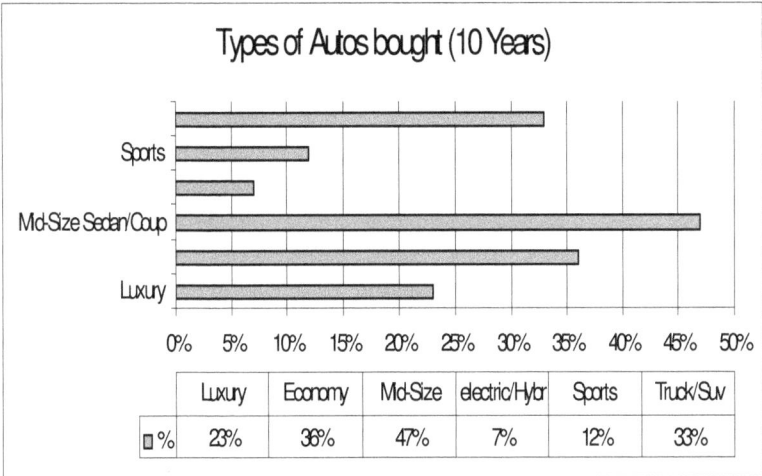

Types of Autos bought (10 Years)

	Luxury	Economy	Mid-Size	electric/Hybr	Sports	Truck/Suv
%	23%	36%	47%	7%	12%	33%

Survey Question #14

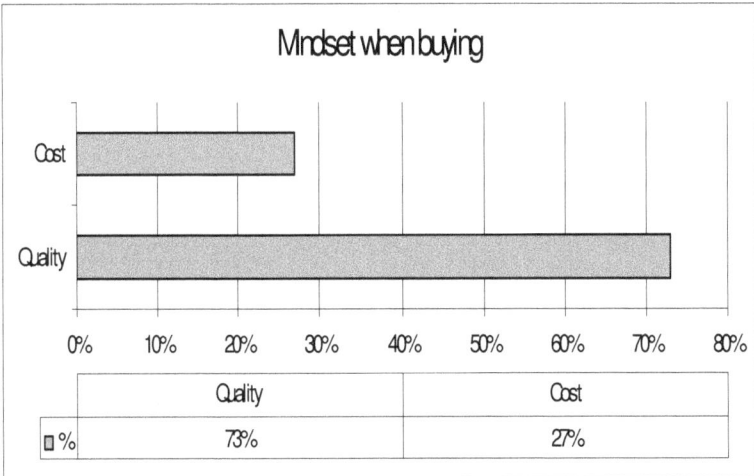

Mindset when buying

	Quality	Cost
%	73%	27%

157

Survey Question #15

Give a Stranger Money?

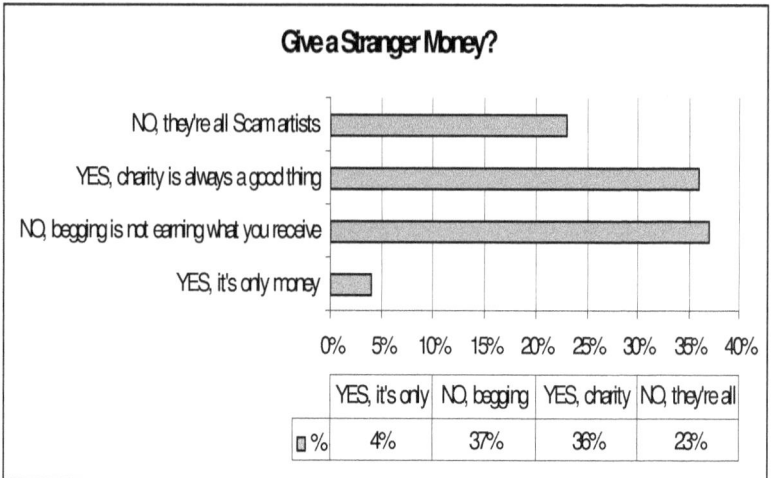

	YES, it's only	NO, begging	YES, charity	NO, they're all
▣%	4%	37%	36%	23%

Survey Question #16

Doggie-Bag for Left Overs

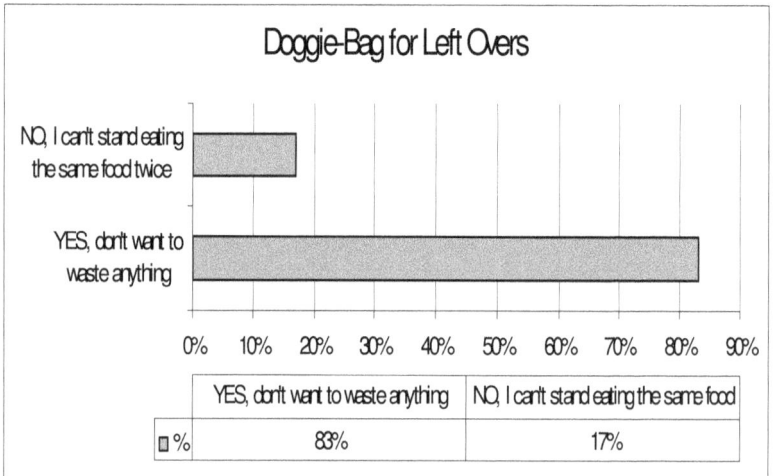

	YES, don't want to waste anything	NO, I can't stand eating the same food
▣%	83%	17%

Survey Question #17(A)

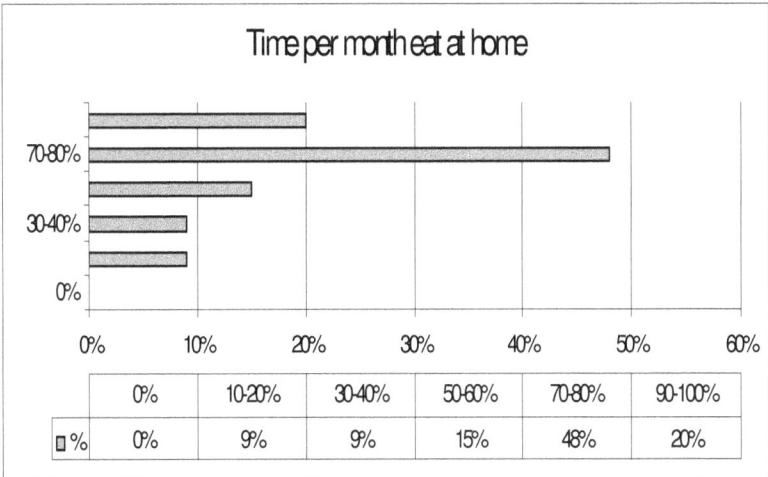

Time per month eat at home

	0%	10-20%	30-40%	50-60%	70-80%	90-100%
%	0%	9%	9%	15%	48%	20%

Survey Question #17(B)

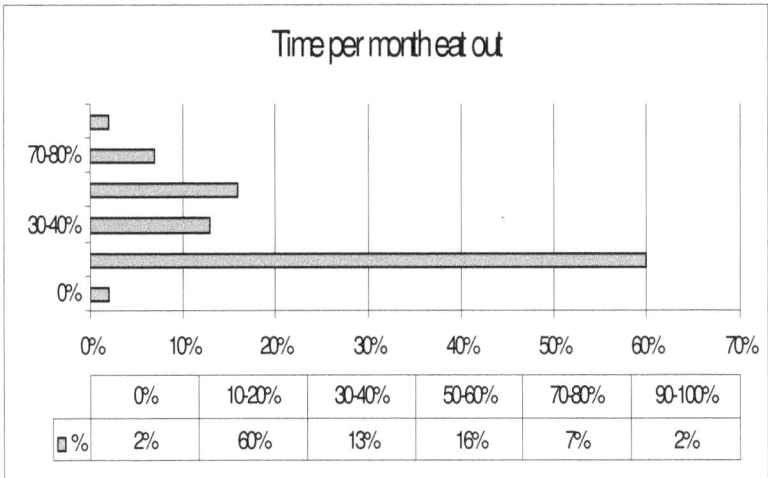

Time per month eat out

	0%	10-20%	30-40%	50-60%	70-80%	90-100%
%	2%	60%	13%	16%	7%	2%

Survey Question #18

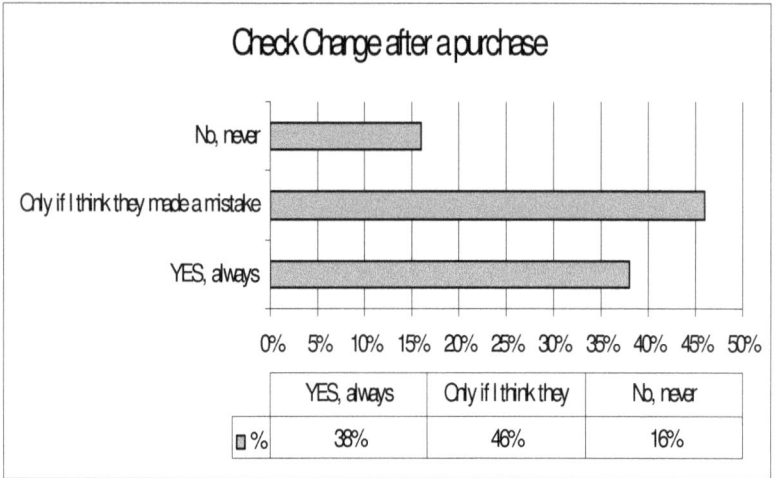

Check Change after a purchase

	YES, always	Only if I think they	No, never
▢ %	38%	46%	16%

Survey Question #19

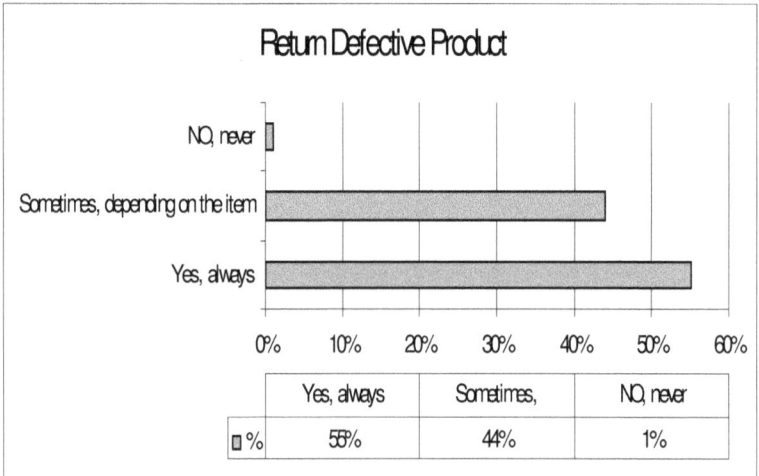

Return Defective Product

	Yes, always	Sometimes,	NO, never
▢ %	55%	44%	1%

www.ingramcontent.com/pod-product-compliance
Lightning Source LLC
Chambersburg PA
CBHW040857210326
41597CB00029B/4883